Essentials of SLA for L2 Teachers

Essentials of SLA for L2 Teachers: A Transdisciplinary Framework presents an accessible and comprehensive account of current understandings of second language acquisition (SLA) geared towards those studying to become L2 teachers. Grounded in the pragmatic and problem-oriented transdisciplinary framework of SLA, this textbook draws connections between SLA research and practices for L2 teaching. It aims to build L2 teacher expertise by strengthening teachers' understandings of the many facets of L2 learning and their skills for designing transformative learning environments in their teaching contexts. The author includes pedagogical implications and inquiry-based activities in each chapter that engage readers in further explorations of the topics covered in the chapter. Short and straightforward, *Essentials of SLA for L2 Teachers* is the ideal main resource for SLA courses taught at undergraduate and graduate-level teaching programs.

Joan Kelly Hall is Professor of Applied Linguistics and Director of the Center for Research on English Language Learning and Teaching at the Pennsylvania State University, USA. She is a member of the Douglas Fir Group who authored the 2016 paper in *The Modern Language Journal* proposing a transdisciplinary framework of SLA on which this text builds.

Essentials of SLA for L2 Teachers

A Transdisciplinary Framework

Joan Kelly Hall

NEW YORK AND LONDON

First published 2019
by Routledge
711 Third Avenue, New York, NY 10017

and by Routledge
2 Park Square, Milton Park, Abingdon, Oxon, OX14 4RN

Routledge is an imprint of the Taylor & Francis Group, an informa business

© 2019 Taylor & Francis

The right of Joan Kelly Hall to be identified as author of this work has been asserted by her in accordance with sections 77 and 78 of the Copyright, Designs and Patents Act 1988.

All rights reserved. No part of this book may be reprinted or reproduced or utilised in any form or by any electronic, mechanical, or other means, now known or hereafter invented, including photocopying and recording, or in any information storage or retrieval system, without permission in writing from the publishers.

Trademark notice: Product or corporate names may be trademarks or registered trademarks, and are used only for identification and explanation without intent to infringe.

Every effort has been made to contact copyright-holders. Please advise the publisher of any errors or omissions, and these will be corrected in subsequent editions.

Library of Congress Cataloging-in-Publication Data
Names: Hall, Joan Kelly, author.
Title: Essentials of SLA for L2 teachers: a transdisciplinary framework / Joan Kelly Hall.
Description: New York, NY: Routledge, [2018] | Includes bibliographical references and index.
Identifiers: LCCN 2018010040 | ISBN 9781138744073 (hardback) | ISBN 9781138744080 (pbk.) |
ISBN 9781351721837 (epub) | ISBN 9781351721820 (mobi/kindle)
Subjects: LCSH: Second language acquisition. | Language and languages—Study and teaching—Foreign speakers.
Classification: LCC P118.2 .H35 2018 | DDC 401/.93—dc23
LC record available at https://lccn.loc.gov/2018010040

ISBN: 978-1-138-74407-3 (hbk)
ISBN: 978-1-138-74408-0 (pbk)
ISBN: 978-1-315-18127-1 (ebk)

Typeset in Sabon
by codeMantra
Printed by CPI Group (UK) Ltd, Croydon CR0 4YY

Contents

Figures viii
Boxes ix
Preface x
Acknowledgements xii

1 **Introduction: A Transdisciplinary Framework of SLA** 1
   Overview 1
   A Transdisciplinary Framework of SLA 3
   Multifaceted Nature of SLA 5
   Themes Deriving from the Transdisciplinary
      Framework of SLA 9
   Summary 14
   Implications for Understanding L2 Teaching: The
      Text's Pedagogical Approach 15
   Pedagogical Activities 16

2 **L2 Knowledge Is Complex and Dynamic** 23
   Overview 23
   What Is Language? 24
   From Linguistic Competence to Multi-Competence 28
   Terms for New Understandings of Language Knowledge 30
   Summary 36
   Implications for Understanding L2 Teaching 36
   Pedagogical Activities 37

3   **L2 Knowledge Is a Repertoire of Diverse Semiotic Resources**   45
    Overview 45
    What Are Semiotic Resources? 45
    Communicative Repertoires 52
    Super-Diverse Communicative Repertoires 53
    Summary 54
    Implications for Understanding L2 Teaching 54
    Pedagogical Activities 55

4   **L2 Learning Is Situated, and Attentionally and Socially Gated**   61
    Overview 61
    Learning Is Situated 61
    Differences Between L1 and L2 Learning 66
    Summary 68
    Implications for Understanding L2 Teaching 68
    Pedagogical Activities 69

5   **L2 Learning Is Mediated and Embodied**   76
    Overview 76
    Language Socialization 76
    Learning How to Mean 82
    Learning Is Mediated and Embodied 83
    Summary 86
    Implications for Understanding L2 Teaching 86
    Pedagogical Activities 88

6   **L2 Learning Is Mediated by Learners' Social Identities**   94
    Overview 94
    Social Identity 94
    Social Identity and L2 Learning 97
    Digital Communication and Changing Identities 100
    Summary 101
    Implications for Understanding L2 Teaching 101
    Pedagogical Activities 103

7   **L2 Learning Is Mediated by Motivation, Investment, and Agency**   109
    Overview 109
    Motivation 109
    Investment 112
    Individual Agency 115

Summary 116
Implications for Understanding L2 Teaching 117
Pedagogical Activities 118

8 **L2 Learning Is Mediated by Literacy and Instructional Practices**   125
Overview 125
Literacy 125
L2 Socialization in Educational Settings 129
Mediational Role of Classroom Interaction 131
Instructional Approaches 136
Summary 138
Implications for Understanding L2 Teaching 139
Pedagogical Activities 140

9 **L2 Learning Is Mediated by Language Ideologies**   152
Overview 152
Language Ideologies 152
Language Policy and Planning 156
Summary 162
Implications for Understanding L2 Teaching 162
Pedagogical Activities 164

Index   171

Figures

1.1	Approaches to SLA represented in the transdisciplinary framework	4
1.2	The multifaceted nature of language learning and teaching	6
1.3	Transdisciplinary understandings of SLA: Eight fundamental themes	10
2.1	Examples of a concept web	39
3.1	Examples of semiotic resources	46
3.2	Semiotic resources of classrooms	51
4.1	Examples of Venn diagrams	70
6.1	Identity chart	103
7.1	Research study summary table	120
8.1	Restricted third turns	132
8.2	Teacher uptake of student responses	133

Boxes

2.1	Concepts: L2 language knowledge is complex and dynamic	38
3.1	On a sign outside of a church	53
3.2	Concepts: L2 knowledge is a repertoire of diverse semiotic resources	57
4.1	Concepts: L2 learning is situated, and attentionally and socially gated	71
5.1	Concepts: L2 learning is mediated and embodied	89
6.1	Concepts: L2 learning is mediated by learners' social identities	104
7.1	Concepts: L2 learning is mediated by motivation, investment, and agency	119
8.1	Concepts: L2 learning is mediated by literacy and instructional practices	141
9.1	Concepts: L2 learning is mediated by language ideologies	165

Preface

This textbook was written to present essential understandings of second language acquisition specifically to L2 teachers. The understandings are organized around a transdisciplinary framework, which, while acknowledging the value of the distinct disciplinary and interdisciplinary approaches to the study of SLA, recognizes that a broader and more grounded perspective of SLA is needed to capture the multifaceted dimensions of SLA. The framework provides such a view by integrating findings on L2 learning arising from various research efforts over three levels of social activity and across time spans.

The framework was developed by a group of 15 scholars, each of whom identifies with a particular approach to SLA. The group's extensive collaborations over an extended period of time resulted in the development of the framework and a publication on the framework for a special issue celebrating 100 years of *The Modern Language Journal* (Douglas Fir Group, 2016, A transdisciplinary framework for SLA in a multilingual world, *The Modern Language Journal*, 100, 19–47). In this text, I expand on the foundational work of the Douglas Fir Group by drawing connections between current understandings of the many dimensions of L2 learning and understandings of L2 teaching.

How Is the Text Organized?

The text is organized around eight themes that cover the micro, meso, and macro levels of social activity. Chapter 1 introduces the framework and each subsequent chapter presents one of the themes. Every chapter includes a chapter abstract, an overview of the material covered in the chapter, a summary of main points, a discussion of implications for understanding L2 teaching derived from the material presented in the chapter, and a set of pedagogical activities that can be undertaken in class, individually, in pairs or small groups, or outside of class, on the reader's own time.

Who Is the Book For?

The text is written specifically for upper-level undergraduate students and MA students pursuing a degree in second or foreign language teaching in institutions around the world. Students who are pursuing degrees in applied linguistics or other related fields or are new to the field of SLA may also find the book valuable. It is not meant to be a comprehensive anthology of research undertaken by the entire field of SLA. Rather, it is offered as a beginning field guide to SLA; it presents a basic introduction to current understandings of language and language learning, which includes concepts that are fundamental to these understandings, and offers considerations on how they inform understandings of L2 teaching.

The goal is to move readers to make connections to their real-life experiences as learners and teachers of languages, to transform their understandings about L2 learning and teaching, and ultimately, to facilitate their development of innovative and sustainable teaching practices that expand their L2 learners' diverse multilingual repertoires of meaning making resources.

Acknowledgements

I am deeply grateful to my fellow members of the Douglas Fir Group for the wide ranging intellectual discussions that led up to the publication of the 2016 co-authored article, which inspired this book. I am also indebted to the following graduate students who read various chapters and offered insightful comments and suggestions: Michael Amory, Yingliang He, Olesya Kisselev, Tianfang (Sally) Wang, and Rebecca Zoshak. Special thanks to my colleague, Karen Johnson, for her collaboration and contributions, and to Yingliang and Sally who provided enormous help in compiling reference lists and from whose copyediting skills I benefited greatly. Finally, I thank the publishing team at Routledge for their patience and support in seeing this project through to completion.

Chapter 1

Introduction
A Transdisciplinary Framework of SLA

Overview

Almost everyone has experienced the learning of a language or languages in addition to their first or native language. For some, the experience may take place in the classroom, where the study of foreign languages is a common subject area offered by schools. Others' first encounters with another language may come from living with caregivers such as grandparents or care providers who speak a language that is different from the dominant language of the community. In these contexts, individuals typically learn different words and phrases in the language of their caregivers to communicate with them about their home-life experiences.

Others may experience language learning by picking up certain words and phrases they encounter while watching television, listening to music, playing video games, or using the internet to find information or communicate with others about shared interests. Still others' experiences with learning another language may happen as friendships are formed with individuals who speak different languages. Understanding how children, adolescents, and adults learn additional languages and the forces that shape the outcomes of their experiences, whether they occur in the classroom, on the internet, or in a myriad of social contexts, is the central concern of the field of *Second Language Acquisition* (SLA).[1]

The SLA field began as an interdisciplinary endeavor in the broader field of Applied Linguistics over half a century ago, with its early research efforts drawing on intellectual developments on language and learning from the fields of linguistics and psychology. The field's strong ties to these disciplines directed SLA's research efforts to concerns with uncovering and explaining the role of cognitive mechanisms in acquiring the structural components of another language. These concerns were mainly limited to language learning by *monolinguals*, i.e., speakers of only one language, who were learning a second language in addition to their first language. This explains the use of the term *second* in the field's name.

As research interests expanded through the 1970s and 1980s, the field recognized that language learners often come to their varied contexts of learning already knowing more than one language. Thus, while the field retained the term *second* in its name, its scope was broadened to include the learning of any additional language, whether it be learners' second, third, or fourth languages, and whether the language is considered a group or community language, a foreign or world language, or an indigenous, minority, or heritage language. The field also uses the term *L2* as an alternative term for *second language*.

Over the last 25 years or so, and particularly since the turn into the twenty-first century, the scope of the field has undergone tremendous growth. The expansion has been fueled in large part by recognition of the need for alternative perspectives that more adequately explain the real-world experiences of L2 learners in modern day society in light of the profound changes brought about by the intersecting forces of globalization, technologization, and large-scale migration. For example, the proliferation of digital technologies such as computers, video games, smart phones, and the internet, has changed the ways in which L2 learners interpret and make meaning, with graphic, pictorial, audio, and spatial patterns of meaning integrated within or even supplanting traditional spoken and written texts.

Together these forces have given rise to communities that are increasingly linguistically, socially, and culturally diverse. Within and across these communities, new and more heterogeneous forms of social activity and options for participating in them that are more diverse, more multilingual, multimodal, and dynamic continue to emerge. In these environments, opportunities for learning additional languages have been expanded and transformed.

L2 learners come to these contexts with diverse social identities marked by varying degrees of access to the activities and their meaning-making resource. L2 learners' varied access to, motivation, and investment in participating in the activities lead to varying developmental trajectories. In some contexts, learners may develop understandings of and skills to use comprehensive and elaborate multilingual resources. In other contexts, L2 learners may develop more specialized resources that are linked to those contexts or they may develop minimal, transitory bits of additional languages, such as isolated greeting patterns, e.g., *hola* from Spanish or *sayonara* from Japanese (Blommaert & Backus, 2011). In other contexts, despite ample access to varied social encounters marked by extensive use of multilingual resources, L2 learners may remain monolingual.

To make sense of the varying processes and outcomes of L2 learning, researchers have looked to other disciplines including anthropology, sociology, and education in addition to areas considered subfields of linguistics and psychology, such as functional linguistics, neurolinguistics, and cultural psychology for insights and research findings. These explorations have resulted in a proliferation of approaches to SLA in addition to the historically dominant cognitive approaches. These approaches range from those that focus on the very micro levels of L2 learning, i.e., the neurobiological and cognitive conditions and outcomes of L2 learning, to the more macro levels, i.e., the sociocultural and ideological structures that both shape and are shaped by L2 learning.

Each of the approaches is characterized by particular research agendas, which, for the most part, are defined by disciplinary concerns that are built on specific disciplinary theories and key concepts. These, in turn, define particular objects of investigation and particular research methods to advance study of the objects. They also specify terminologies to refer to the objects of study and value certain methods of investigation over others, the purpose of which is to advance new hypotheses about the formal properties of the theories and concepts. Their theories, concepts, and methods give shape both to the directions that research projects take and their outcomes.

Arguing for engagement across perspectives to advance the field, some SLA scholars from these different approaches have come together to explore concepts from different perspectives, such as the nature of language and learning. One well-known exploration is Dwight Atkinson's (2011) volume entitled *Alternative Approaches to Second Language Acquisition*, in which six complementary perspectives on L2 learning are presented. While these efforts have made great contributions to the advancement of theoretical and conceptual understandings about language and learning, for the most part, their intellectual energies have remained on disciplinary concerns. Their capacity for providing solutions to the real-world challenges of L2 learning in modern day society has been less effective. This is due in large part to the fact that the challenges of L2 learning are highly complex, varying across individuals, across groups and across communities. Practical, participant-relevant and sustainable responses to these challenges cannot be construed from only one or two disciplinary perspectives.

A Transdisciplinary Framework of SLA

To meet the challenges of addressing the real-world issues of L2 learning, a new intellectual framework for the field of SLA has emerged (Douglas Fir Group, 2016). Termed *transdisciplinary*, the framework was developed by a group of 15 scholars, each member of which identifies with a particular disciplinary or interdisciplinary approach to SLA, and whose extensive collaborations over an extended period of time resulted in the development of the framework. The approaches to SLA represented in

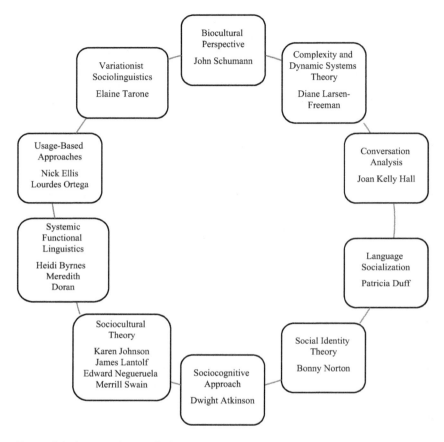

Figure 1.1 Approaches to SLA represented in the transdisciplinary framework.

the transdisciplinary framework include the biocultural perspective, complexity and dynamic systems theory, conversation analysis, language socialization, social identity theory, the sociocognitive approach, sociocultural theory, systemic functional linguistics, usage-based approaches, and variationist sociolinguistics. These are displayed in Figure 1.1 and each approach includes the names of SLA scholars comprising the Douglas Fir Group who represent it.

At its center, the transdisciplinary framework is pragmatic and problem-oriented. While it acknowledges the value of the distinct disciplinary and interdisciplinary perspectives, it recognizes that a broader, and at the same time, more grounded perspective of SLA is needed to capture the whole project of SLA in all its multifaceted complexity. It provides such a view by synthesizing findings on L2 learning arising from the various research efforts across disciplines and over many different levels of detail and time spans.

The framework presented in this text expands on the foundational work of the Douglas Fir Group (2016) and adds to their efforts by drawing connections between current understandings of the many dimensions of L2 learning and understandings of and practices for doing L2 teaching. Its goal is twofold. First, it aims to advance understandings of the ever-changing landscapes of L2 learners' social worlds that are ecologically valid (Cicourel, 2007). Understandings that are ecologically valid are *fair* and *credible* representations of "the possibilities and constraints faced by L2 learners in their social worlds on all levels of activity and across time spans" (Douglas Fir Group, 2016, p. 39). The second goal is to create deeper, more nuanced understandings of L2 learning that can inform L2 teachers' development of practical, innovative, and sustainable solutions for expanding L2 learners' diverse multilingual repertoires of meaning-making resources across a range of social contexts and over their lifespan. In the next section, we summarize the multifaceted, dynamic nature of SLA.

Multifaceted Nature of SLA

Foundational to the transdisciplinary framework is the understanding that SLA is a complex, on-going, multidimensional phenomenon involving the dynamic and variable interplay among a range of individual internal cognitive capabilities on the one hand and, on the other, L2 learners' diverse experiences in their multilingual worlds (Douglas Fir Group, 2016). From their experiences, L2 learners develop variable repertoires of multilingual semiotic resources (Hall, Cheng & Carlson, 2006; Blommaert & Backus, 2011). Semiotic resources are an open set of ever-evolving multilingual and multimodal means by which meanings are made in social contexts of action. They include a wide array of linguistic constructions in addition to nonverbal, visual, graphic, and auditory modes of meaning making. The dynamic multidimensional nature of SLA is illustrated in Figure 1.2. As shown, three mutually dependent layers of social activity shape L2 learning.

Micro Level

At the micro level of social activity, L2 learners draw on various internal mechanisms and capacities as they interact with others in a multiplicity of social contexts. The scope of these contexts can be wide-ranging, and may include everyday, informal contexts of interaction, such as personal conversations with family members and friends enacted in face-to-face

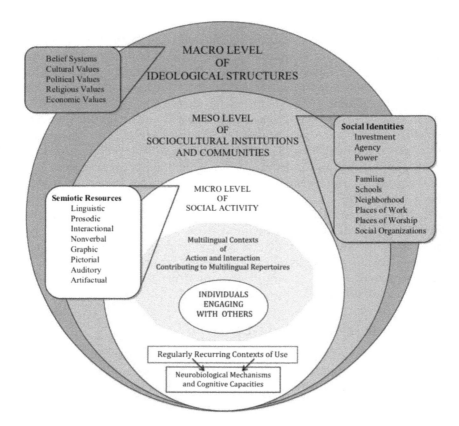

Figure 1.2 The multifaceted nature of language learning and teaching.
Source: Douglas Fir Group (2016, p. 25).

encounters or via technological means such as cellphones and the internet. They can also include ad hoc social conversations with neighbors and work mates. Interactions may also include more formal contexts such as those found in educational or workplace settings where many interactions are undertaken for instructional or professional purposes.

These encounters can be highly routinized in that the goals of the interaction, the roles of participants, and the semiotic resources are very familiar to all involved. Other interactions may be less routine or familiar. Entering workplaces as new employees can present L2 learners with new, unfamiliar contexts of interaction. Likewise, traveling to different geographical regions may involve L2 learners in a diversity of contexts of interaction. In some cases, they may be familiar contexts, e.g., service encounters such as those that occur in stores and restaurants, but the expectations for how to take action and the resources used to make meaning in these actions will be new. In other cases, the contexts and goals and roles of participants may be entirely new.

In their interactions with others in their varied contexts of social action, L2 learners draw on a set of neurobiological and cognitive and emotional capacities with which all human beings are endowed. These include social cognitive skills that drive individuals to seek cooperative interaction with others and general cognitive capabilities that make possible the processing of information. These capabilities guide learners in selecting and attending to particular meaning-making semiotic resources and their patterns of use and in forming schemas based on the recurrences of the resources in their encounters. They also guide learners in creating mappings across resources based on functional similarities, and to hypothesize about and continually test their understandings of and abilities to use the resources in context-sensitive ways.

Supporting L2 learners' cognitive processes are cues used by others that help to make transparent the patterned uses of semiotic resources and assist learners in noticing and remembering them. Such assistance can involve a range of resources that explicitly direct learners' attention to the relevant semiotic resources and their meaning-making potentials, and other less explicit actions such as, for example, repetitions, tone and pitch changes to speech, and eye gaze and gestures. In classrooms for example, such work is typically accomplished via an assemblage of instructional actions that direct learners to perceive or notice the relevant resources and to make connections between them and their contexts of use. The more routine, frequent, and stable the occurrences of particular resources are in L2 learners' interactions with others, and the more learners' attention is drawn to their form-meaning pairings, the more entrenched the resources become as cognitive representations of their experiences. Variations in L2 learners' experiences lead to the development of varied multilingual repertoires of semiotic resources, each which is linked to different social contexts and in continuous adaptation to its use (Bybee & Hopper, 2001). All else being equal, the more extensive and complex the contexts of interaction become over time and the more enduring L2 learners' participation is in them, the more complex and enduring their multilingual repertoires will be.

Meso Level

The sociocultural institutions within which L2 learners' contexts of interactions are situated constitute the meso level of social activity. These institutions include the family, neighborhoods, schools, and places of work and worship. Also included are social and community organizations such as clubs, sports leagues, political parties, various online contexts, and so on.

L2 learners' institutions and their particular contexts of interaction are shaped by pervasive social, cultural, economic, political, and other conditions. These conditions not only influence the types of contexts of interactions that are enacted in them, but also shape the particular attitudes, perspectives, motives, and values that are embodied in the contexts of interaction. In schools, for example, some contexts of interaction are perceived to have more value than others. In some social groups, student self-initiation and active participation are highly valued while in others such actions break the social norms of group conformity and are seen as a challenge to teacher authority. These perceptions and values are historically derived, developed over time and tied to particular social groups with the authority to shape them (Heath, 1983; Hymes, 1980). Often invisible, this authority derives from various levels of social, political, and economic powers.

Contexts of interactions constituting L2 learners' social institutions, along with their attendant perspectives, attitudes, motives, and values can and, in fact, do vary within and across geographical regions, and in some cases, they vary quite widely. What may be considered appropriate contexts of interaction in an institution of one community, for example, may be considered inappropriate or even highly unsuitable in that of another community. These variations can lead to differences in the development of L2 learners' repertoires of semiotic resources.

The widespread social, cultural, other conditions tied to the various sociocultural institutions also shape learners' social identities. Social identities are aspects of L2 learners' personhoods that are defined in terms of the various social groups into which they are born, including, for example, groups defined by ethnicity, race, social class, nationality, and religion (Ochs, 1996). They also have a second layer of social identities, defined by the role relationships they create or are assigned to in the various contexts of interactions of their social institutions. In families, for example, individuals take on roles as parents, children, siblings, and interact with others, as, for example, mothers to daughters, brothers to sisters, or husbands to wives. Likewise, in the workplace, L2 learners interact with others in their roles as, for example, supervisors, managers, subordinates, or colleagues.

Learners' social identities and the groups they belong to are significant to the development of their multilingual repertoires in that they define in part the kinds of contexts of interaction and the particular semiotic resources for accomplishing them to which they have access. For example, in some regions of the world, depending on their race or social class, some L2 learners may find the L2 learning opportunities they have access to are limited or constrained while others may find their opportunities to be abundant and unrestrained (Collins, 2014).

All else being equal, the greater the number and diversity of contexts of interaction within and across social institutions that L2 learners are given access to and are motivated to participate in, the richer and more linguistically diverse the semiotic resources of these contexts are, and the more extended their opportunities are for deriving form-meaning patterns of these meaning-making resources, the more robust their multilingual repertoires arising from their experiences are likely to be compared to those of L2 learners with fewer and less varied experiences.

Macro Level

Ideological structures constitute the macro level of social activity. Ideologies are individual- and group-shared beliefs and values about the form and influence of culture, politics, religion, and economics on all levels of social activity (Kroskrity, 2010). Often invisible and taken for granted, the beliefs and values influence the ways that individuals and groups view their worlds and act within them and the ways they interpret the actions of others.

Ideologies about language use and language learning are especially significant to SLA endeavors, influencing language policy and planning on all levels of social activity. For example, they shape decisions on which language or languages are official, how they are to be used in various institutional settings and the opportunities that are made available to individual L2 learners, as members of their social groups, to learn, use and maintain these languages (Farr & Song, 2011). Beliefs and values at the macro level are in constant interaction with the other levels of social activity, and may vary and even be contradictory within and across individuals, groups, contexts of interaction, and social institutions.

While each of the three levels of social activity has its distinguishing features, no level exists on its own, apart from the others. Each exists only through constant, dynamic interaction with the others, with each level of activity shaping and being shaped by the others. Understanding the cognitive and social conditions giving shape to L2 learning at each level is essential to understanding the whole project of SLA.

Themes Deriving from the Transdisciplinary Framework of SLA

Eight fundamental themes about the nature of language and learning can be derived from the three interdependent levels of social activity.[2] Each theme offers action possibilities for L2 research, L2 learning, and L2 teaching. These themes are represented in Figure 1.3. As shown in the figure, no one theme is more important than another nor are they categorical. Rather, they are interdependent, overlapping and in dialogue

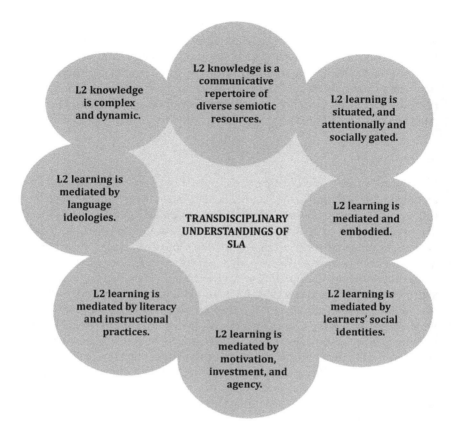

Figure 1.3 Transdisciplinary understandings of SLA: Eight fundamental themes.

with each other. Below, each of the eight themes is summarized. These themes, their attendant concepts and understandings, and their implications for understanding L2 teaching are covered more deeply in subsequent chapters of the text.

Theme 1: L2 Knowledge Is Complex and Dynamic

This theme addresses the composition of language knowledge. In contrast to a view of language knowledge as an unchanging, fixed system of abstract structures, a transdisciplinary perspective understands it to be a dynamic, open-ended collection of varied resources for making meaning (Bybee & Hopper, 2001; Halliday, 1975, 1993; Hymes, 1972a, 1972b). The collections of resources that comprise L2 learners' knowledge develop from their experiences in contexts of interaction as they go about doing "the communicative work humans do" (Bybee & Hopper, 2001, p. 3). This means that to *learn* another language one must be involved in contexts of interaction *using* the language. All else being equal, the salient resources by which the contexts of interaction are accomplished are the resources that eventually become appropriated by the learner. Any appearance of stability in L2 learners' language knowledge is a matter of stability in their social experiences, with similar resources across users reflecting "historically popular solutions to similar communicative and coordination problems" (Ibbotson, 2012, p. 124).

Theme 2: L2 Knowledge Is a Repertoire of Diverse Semiotic Resources

Addressed in this theme is the transdisciplinary understanding of L2 knowledge as more than just linguistic resources. In fact, it comprises a wide range of semiotic resources for making meaning that include nonverbal, visual, graphic, and auditory modes (Kress, 2009). All semiotic resources, individually and in combination, have conventionalized form-meaning combinations that develop from their past uses in particular contexts of action which, in turn, are shaped by forces at both the meso and macro levels of social activity.

In response to criticisms that using the term *competence* to refer to the collection of semiotic resources that L2 learners know carries an ideology that implies homogeneity and permanence (Blommaert & Rampton, 2011; Hall, 2016; Makoni & Pennycook, 2007), a transdisciplinary perspective uses the term *repertoire* to capture the dynamic, malleable nature of individual L2 knowledge. The greater the number and diversity of contexts of interaction within and across social institutions that L2 learners are given access to, and are motivated to participate in, the richer and more diverse their repertoires of semiotic resources will be.

Theme 3: L2 Learning Is Situated, and Attentionally and Socially Gated

This theme deals with the situated nature of L2 learning. As noted earlier, L2 learning begins at the micro-level of social activity, through L2 learners' repeated experiences in situated, regularly occurring contexts of interaction. In their interactions, they draw on a set of cognitive capabilities that interact with the properties of the input to give shape to their repertoires. These include capabilities to select and attend to particular meaning-making components and their patterns of action, to form representations based on their recurrences, to create mappings across units based on functional similarities, and to hypothesize about and continually test their understandings of their meanings.

Key aspects of the input that interact with these capabilities are the distribution and frequency with which particular semiotic resources are encountered. The more frequent the occurrence of different semiotic resources and the more learners' attention is drawn to them, the more entrenched they become as cognitive representations of L2 knowledge. Conversely, the less frequent the occurrences of the resources are or the less noticeable they are to L2 learners, the more weakly these resources are represented in learners' L2 knowledge (Ibbotson, 2013).

Theme 4: L2 Learning Is Mediated and Embodied

Theme 4 addresses the social nature of L2 learning processes. Supporting learners' cognitive processes in noticing, ordering, representing, and remembering their involvement in their contexts of interaction are cues used by others, typically more experienced participants, which indicate or call attention to the form–meaning patterns and assist L2 learners in noticing and remembering them (Dabrowska, 2012; Ellis & Larsen-Freeman, 2006; Tomasello, 2003, 2008). The cues can take many forms, including verbal and nonverbal instructions that explicitly direct L2 learners' attention to particular resources and their meanings. They can also be less explicit cues such as repetitions, sound changes as one speaks, eye gazes, and gestures; they can include computational resources such as computers and calculators, graphic resources such as diagrams, maps and drawings, and writing systems. It is often the case that multiple embodied modes are used simultaneously. One can point while speaking, for example, or gesture to an illustration to prompt learners' attention. Another way to refer to the action of using cues to draw learners' attention to aspects of their contexts of interaction is *mediation*. Learning is mediated by the use of various multimodal, semiotic resources as L2 learners move through, respond to, and make sense of their social worlds (Scollon, 2001; Vygotsky, 1978; Wertsch, 1994).

Theme 5: L2 Learning Is Mediated by Learners' Social Identities

This theme is concerned with the variable role that learners' social identities play in L2 learning. L2 learners come to their contexts of interaction as actors with multiple intersecting, sometimes conflicting, social identities. The social institutions of their groups and communities not only influence social expectations for how L2 learners' social identities are enacted and the semiotic resources they have access to; they also influence learners' motivations for seeking out and pursuing interactions with others.

In addition to their actual social identities, L2 learners' *imagined* social identities and group memberships can influence their access to particular social institutions and contexts of interaction within them (Pavlenko & Norton, 2007; Norton, 2000; Norton & Toohey, 2011). Imagined identities and social group memberships are those that learners desire to assume or adopt because they perceive that such group memberships can offer them greater access to a wider range of "socially constituted repertoires of identificational and affiliational resources" (Bauman, 2000, p. 1) and opportunities for interaction. These in turn, they anticipate, will afford them greater economic and/or social stability. Moreover, through varying degrees of access to and memberships of their real and desired social groups and role relationships, new identities may become available to them, further shaping their opportunities for expanding their L2 repertoires. For example, refugees are often positioned to enter the unskilled or low-wage labor force despite the professional qualifications they bring with them from their home countries. They will most likely need to resist this positioning if they are to gain access to opportunities in which they will be able to achieve both personal and professional goals. For all L2 learners, their expanding repertoires will, in turn, influence the identities and the means for enacting them they will have access to (Norton, 2013).

Theme 6: L2 learning Is Mediated by Motivation, Investment, and Agency

Theme 6 deals with the roles that motivation, investment, and individual agency play in the learning process. While learners' L2 repertoires are to a great extent shaped by social institutional expectations about their group memberships, as individual agents they also play a role in shaping them. For example, in contexts of interaction where L2 learners struggle to participate from one identity position, they may be able to act independently from some factors of influence and create or take on different identities and social roles. Such agentive moves can serve to change their access and opportunities to use particular resources and to participating in particular contexts of interaction (Higgins, 2015; Morita, 2004; Norton & Toohey, 2011; Rampton, 2013). However, the degree of individual effort L2 learners can exert in shaping their identities is not equal across contexts. Rather, it is "an aspect of the action" (Altieri, 1994, p. 4), negotiable in and arising from the particular social, political, economic, and other forces that give shape to the social institutions and by extension L2 learners' local contexts of interaction.

Theme 7: L2 Learning Is Mediated by Literacy and Instructional Practices

Theme 7 discusses the influential role of literacy and instructional practices in shaping learners' L2 repertoires. Like the other factors involved in shaping L2 learning, the types of literacy and instructional practices that L2 learners engage in over extended periods of time can vary, and in some cases quite widely. The degrees of variation in the types of practices and the resources used to accomplish them along with the varying paths that learners' socialization into them take lead to variations in the development of learners' L2 repertoires. The empirical understandings of the links between variations in these practices and L1 learning are undisputed; empirical knowledge about their influences on L2 learning are only beginning to be fully understood.

Theme 8: L2 Learning Is Mediated by Language Ideologies

Theme 8 is concerned with the influence of language ideologies on L2 learning. Language ideologies (beliefs, feelings, and conceptions about language) are especially significant to the endeavors of L2 learning. They shape not only the contexts of interaction and semiotic resources that L2 learners have access to but also learners' investment in their and others' social identities and their motivation for engaging with others in their contexts of interaction (Ricento, 2000; Tollefson, 2002).

These ideologies influence language policies on all levels of social activity. They give shape to decisions on which language or languages are official, which languages and language varieties are valued, and the educational opportunities that are made available to individuals to learn and use them (De Costa, 2010; Farr & Song, 2011; Hult, 2014). A particularly damaging language ideology to L2 learning is the belief that monolingualism is the "default for the human capacity for language" (Ortega, 2014, p. 35) and thus the standard against which language use is judged. It can function to create negative social, academic, and personal evaluations of L2 learners and of any language not considered to be the official or standard language. Understanding how these beliefs about language, which are often invisible, influence L2 learning at all levels of SLA is critical to understanding the whole enterprise of SLA.

Summary

The transdisciplinary framework presented here offers an integrated representation of the multilayered complexity of SLA. It is on the micro-level of social interaction where L2 learning begins, with L2 learners' repertoires of semiotic resources emerging from continual interaction between internal biological and cognitive capacities on the one hand and their trajectories of experiences in specific contexts of interaction on the other. Their experiences, in turn, are shaped by larger social institutional contexts whose structures of expectations influence not only the scope and scale of L2 learners' social experiences and the meaning potentials of their semiotic resources. They also give shape to learners' social identities, which can lead to varied opportunities for access to their experiences. At the macro level, these institutional expectations are influenced by larger, more persistent forces and ideologies, which make possible and, at the same time, are made possible by social activity on all levels. The dynamic and malleable repertoires of resources that L2 learners develop from their real-world experiences over their lifespans are cognitive in that they are represented in learners' minds as relatively automatized, functionally distributed, and context-sensitive collections of semiotic resources. They are, at the same time, social in that the development of individual repertoires is tied to learners' varied experiences in multilingual contexts of action within and across all sociocultural institutions. Variations in conditions at all levels of social activity, from the very micro scale of social life to large-scale social ideologies lead to dynamic and varied trajectories of L2 development and, ultimately to learners with dynamic, varied multilingual repertoires. The eight themes deriving from the transdisciplinary framework of SLA along with their implications for L2 teaching are discussed in greater depth in subsequent chapters.

Implications for Understanding L2 Teaching: The Text's Pedagogical Approach

We believe that for the transdisciplinary framework for SLA to be relevant to the work of language teachers it must be grounded in the actual activities of becoming and being a language teacher. In addition, the framework must be made accessible in ways that facilitate, i.e., mediate, teachers' reevaluation of their understandings of and skills for teaching such that the content of their instruction is relevant, usable, and accessible to their students.

In line with these goals, the pedagogical activities found at the end of each chapter are adapted from Cope and Kalantiz's (2000, 2009, 2015) reflexive approach to pedagogy and curriculum. Originating from the New London Group's (1996) "A Pedagogy of Multiliteracies", reflexive pedagogy is deliberate teaching that engages learners in moving between and among different ways of knowing, connecting to their own experiences, and applying their learning to their social worlds. The different ways of knowing are what Cope and Kalantzis have labeled *knowledge processes*. A knowledge process is an activity type that represents a distinct way of making knowledge.

The four knowledge processes around which pedagogical activities are organized at the end of each chapter are labeled *experiencing*, *conceptualizing, analyzing,* and *applying,* and each knowledge process is subsequently distinguished by two interconnected processes as illustrated below.

Experiencing:
- the known – learners reflect on their own familiar experiences, interests and perspectives
- the new – learners observe or take part in something that is unfamiliar; they are immersed in new situations or content.

Conceptualizing:
- by naming – learners group things into categories, label them with abstract terms, and define these terms
- with theory – learners make generalizations using concepts, and connect terms in concept maps or theories.

Analyzing:
- functionally – learners analyze logical connections, cause and effect, structure and function
- critically – learners evaluate their own and other people's perspectives, interests, and motives.

Applying:
- appropriately – learners apply new learning to real-world situations and test their validity
- creatively – learners make an intervention in the world which is innovative and creative, or transfer their learning to a different context.

The four dimensions of knowledge processes do not represent rigid, ordered stages of learning. Rather, they are complexly interrelated, "elements of each [which] may occur simultaneously, while at different times one or the other will predominate, and all of them are repeatedly revisited at different levels" (New London Group, 2000, p. 85). Together, the activities support teachers' use of conceptual and informational resources of a transdisciplinary framework of SLA to reframe and/or reconstruct their own personal experiences as L2 learners, L2 users, and developing L2 teachers.

Pedagogical Activities

In each chapter, you will engage in a series of pedagogical activities that are organized around the four knowledge processes. The activities can be completed in writing or orally, and individually or in small groups, or in some combination of both. In the pedagogical activities for this chapter, you will engage in different knowledge processes that will assist you in relating to and making sense of the conceptual and informational resources of a transdisciplinary framework of SLA covered in this chapter.

Experiencing

A. Language Learning Experiences

Reflect on your own language learning experiences. These may be in language classrooms, with family or friends, while traveling or living in a new country or culture, or work related. Reflect on what was unique about these experiences and why. Then select one experience that was particularly memorable and create a visual depiction that captures the essence of this experience for you as a language learner. With your classmates, in pairs or small groups, or in a reflection paper, describe what was unique about this language learning experience and why.

B. Language Learning Experiences

Imagine a language learning experience that you have not encountered before but would like to and consider the following questions.

- What might be the social, cultural, academic, and/or professional setting for this experience?
- What would you expect to happen during this experience?
- What would you like to accomplish through this experience?

Create a visual depiction that captures the essence of this experience for you as a language learner. In pairs or small groups, or in a reflection paper, describe your imagined language learning experience and why you have framed it as you have.

Conceptualizing

A. Three Levels of Social Activity

Examine both visual depictions that you created according to the distinguishing features that make up the micro, meso, and macro levels of social activity as defined in this chapter. In pairs or small groups, or in a reflection paper, describe the sociocultural institutions and communities in which each takes place, explain the ideological structures that are most salient, and identify the most routinized patterns of social activity.

B. Three Levels of Social Activity

Examine both visual depictions, identify any connections that emerge between the micro, meso, and macro levels of social activity, and then consider the following:

- What effect might particular ideologies about language have on how particular semiotic resources are utilized at the micro level of social activity?
- Conversely, how might the use of particular semiotic resources reflect the beliefs systems that are apparent at the macro level?

Analyzing

A. Fundamental Themes of a Transdisciplinary Framework

Analyze both visual depictions for evidence of the eight themes presented in this chapter. Select three or four themes that you believe are most salient in both your actual and imagined language learning experiences. They may be the same themes or different ones. Write a reflection paper in which you describe how you have experienced each of these themes in your actual language learning experiences. Compare these themes to those you might experience in your imagined language learning experiences.

B. Language Learning Experiences

Create a list of the most salient similarities and differences between your actual and imagined language learning experiences. In pairs or in small groups, consider the following questions:

- What do these similarities and differences suggest about the multifaceted nature of SLA?
- What do these similarities and differences suggest about the varied trajectories of L2 language development?

Applying

A. Fundamental Themes of a Transdisciplinary Framework

Select one of the eight fundamental themes and design a mini-inquiry project in which you investigate and report on evidence of how this theme plays out in a real-world situation.

For example: Theme 1: L2 Knowledge Is Complex and Dynamic

Observe at least five patrons involved in a typical service encounter in a real-world setting (ordering coffee in a coffee shop, etc.). Take field notes on both the routinized and idiosyncratic ways in which patrons and servers use language to accomplish this service encounter. Write a paper in which you report on what you observed and articulate what you believe your observations suggest about the complex and dynamic nature of language.

B. Fundamental Themes of a Transdisciplinary Framework

Based on the findings of your mini-inquiry project, create an instructional activity for a particular group of L2 learners, in a particular instructional context that will enable them to develop an awareness of how this theme plays out in a real-world situation.

For example: Theme 1: L2 Knowledge Is Complex and Dynamic

Create three different dialogues that depict a typical service encounter in a real-world setting (e.g., ordering coffee in a coffee shop, etc.). Ask the group of L2 students to compare and contrast the three dialogues noting in particular the various ways in which language is used to accomplish each encounter. Have the students report on what they noticed and articulate what they believe their observations suggest about the complex and dynamic nature of language.

Notes

1 SLA's object of inquiry has been and continues to be the learning of languages "at any point in the life span *after* the learning of one or more languages has taken place in the context of primary socialization in the family; in most societies this means prior to formal schooling and sometimes in the absence of literacy mediation" (Douglas Fir, 2016, p. 21). Although concerned with the study of additional languages as well, studies of bilingual first language acquisition (BFLA), i.e., "language development among infants and children when they grow up surrounded by two or more languages" (Ortega, 2011, p. 171), have historically remained outside the main purview of SLA and dealt with, instead, in the field of *bilingualism*.
2 These themes are adaptations of the ten themes formulated by the Douglas Fir Group (2016).

References

Altieri, C. (1994). *Subjective agency*. Cambridge, MA: Blackwell.
Atkinson, D. (2011). *Alternative approaches to second language acquisition*, 1st ed. New York: Routledge.
Bauman, R. (2000). Language, identity, performance. *Pragmatics, 10*, 1–5.
Blommaert, J., & Backus, A. (2011). Repertoires revisited: "Knowing language" in superdiversity. *Working Papers in Urban Language & Literacies, 67*. Accessed 23 July 2012 at www.kcl.ac.uk/sspp/departments/education/research/ldc/publications/workingpapers/67.pdf.
Blommaert, J., & Rampton, B. (2011). Language and superdiversity. In *Diversities, 13*, Accessed 9 February 2014 at http://unesdoc.unesco.org/images/0021/002147/214772e.pdf#214780.
Bybee, J., & Hopper, P. (2001). Introduction to frequency and the emergence of linguistic structure. In J. Bybee & P. Hopper (Eds.), *Frequency and the emergence of linguistic structure* (pp. 1–24). Philadelphia/Amsterdam: John Benjamins.
Cicourel, A. (2007). A personal, retrospective view of ecological validity. *Text & Talk, 27*, 735–752.
Collins, J. (2014). Literacy practices, linguistic anthropology and social inequality. *Working Papers in Urban Language & Literacies, 143*. Accessed 15 November 2014 at www.academia.edu/9277086/WP143_Collins_2014._Literacy_practices_linguistic_anthropology_and_social_inequality.
Cope, B., & Kalantzis, M. (Eds.) (2000). *Multiliteracies: Literacy learning and the design of social futures*. London: Routledge.
Cope, B., & Kalantzis, M. (2009). "Multiliteracies"; New literacies, new learning. *Pedagogies: An International Journal, 4*(3), 164–195.
Cope, B., & Kalantiz, M. (Eds.) (2015). *A pedagogy of multiliteracies: Learning by design*. New York: Palgrave Macmillan.
Dabrowska, E. (2012). Different speakers, different grammars: Individual differences in native language attainment. *Linguistic Approaches to Bilingualism, 2*, 219–225.
De Costa, P. I. (2010). Reconceptualizing language, language learning, and the adolescent immigrant language learner in the age of postmodern globalization. *Language and Linguistics Compass, 4*, 769–781.
Douglas Fir Group (2016). A transdisciplinary framework for SLA in a multilingual world. *The Modern Language Journal, 100*, 19–47.
Ellis, N. C., & Larsen-Freeman, D. (2006). Language emergence: Implications for applied linguistics. Introduction to the Special Issue. *Applied Linguistics, 27*, 558–589.
Farr, M., & Song, J. (2011). Language ideologies and policies: Multilingualism and education. *Language and Linguistics Compass, 5*, 650–665.
Hall, J. K. (2016) A usage-based view of multicompetence. In V. Cook & W. Li. (Eds.), *Cambridge handbook of linguistic multicompetence* (pp. 183–206). Cambridge: Cambridge University Press.
Hall, J. K., Cheng, A., & Carlson, M. T. (2006). Reconceptualizing multicompetence as a theory of language knowledge. *Applied Linguistics, 27*, 220–240.
Halliday, M. A. K. (1975). *Learning how to mean: Explorations in the development of language*. London: Edward Arnold.

Halliday, M. A. K. (1993). Toward a language-based theory of learning. *Linguistics and Education*, 5, 93–116.
Heath, S. B. (1983). *Ways with words: Language, life, and work in communities and in classrooms*. Cambridge: Cambridge University Press.
Higgins, C. (2015). Intersecting scapes and new millennium identities in language learning. *Language Teaching*, 48(3), 373–389.
Hult, F. (2014). How does policy influence language in education? In R. Silver & S. Lwin (Eds.), *Language in education: Social implications* (pp. 159–175). London: Continuum.
Hymes, D. (1972a). On communicative competence. In J. B. Pride & J. Holmes (Eds.), *Sociolinguistics* (pp. 269–293). Harmondsworth: Penguin.
Hymes, D. (1972b). Models of the interaction of language and social life. In J. J. Gumperz & D. Hymes (Eds.), *Directions in sociolinguistics: The ethnography of communication* (pp. 35–71). New York: Holt, Rinehart & Winston.
Hymes, D. (1980). *Language in education: Ethnolinguistic essays*. Washington DC: Center for Applied Linguistics.
Ibbotson, P. (2012). A new kind of language. *The Psychologist*, 25, 122–125.
Ibbotson, P. (2013). The scope of usage-based theory. *Frontiers in Psychology*, 4, 1–15.
Kress. G. (2009). *Multimodality: A social semiotic approach to contemporary communication*. New York: Routledge/Taylor & Francis.
Kroskrity, P. (2010). Language ideologies. In J-O. Ostman & J. Verschueren (Eds.), *Handbook of pragmatics* (pp. 1–24). Philadelphia/Amsterdam: John Benjamins.
Lee, N., Mikesell, L., Joaquin, A. D. L., Mates, A. W., & Schumann, J. H. (2009). *The interactional instinct: The evolution and acquisition of language*. Oxford: Oxford University Press.
Makoni, S., & Pennycook, A. (Eds.) (2007). *Disinventing and reconstituting languages*. Clevedon: Multilingual Matters.
Morita, N. (2004). Negotiating participation and identity in second language academic communities. *TESOL Quarterly*, 38, 573–603.
New London Group (1996). A pedagogy of multiliteracies: Designing social futures. *Harvard Educational Review*, 66, 60–92.
Norton, B. (2000). *Identity and language learning*. Harlow: Pearson Education.
Norton, B. (2013). Identity and second language acquisition. In C. Chapelle (Ed.), *Encyclopedia of applied linguistics*. Wiley-Blackwell.
Norton, B., & Toohey, K. (2011). Identity, language learning, and social change. *Language Teaching*, 44, 412–446.
Ochs, E. (1996). Linguistic resources for socializing humanity In J. J. Gumperz & S. Levinson (Eds.), *Rethinking linguistic relativity* (pp. 407–437). Cambridge: Cambridge University Press.
Ortega, L. (2011). SLA after the social turn: Where cognitivism and its alternatives stand. In D. Atkinson (Ed.), *Alternative approaches in second language acquisition* (pp. 167–180). New York: Routledge.
Ortega, L. (2014). Ways forward for a bi/multilingual turn in SLA. In S. May (Ed.), *The multilingual turn: Implications for SLA, TESOL and bilingual education* (pp. 32–52). New York: Routledge.
Pavlenko, A., & Norton, B. (2007). Imagined communities, identity, and English language teaching. In J. Cummins & C. Davison (Eds.), *International handbook of English language teaching* (pp. 669–680). New York: Springer.

Rampton, B. (2013). Styling in a language learned later in life. *The Modern Language Journal, 97,* 360–382.

Ricento, T. (2000). Historical and theoretical perspectives in language policy and planning. *Journal of Sociolinguistics, 4,* 196–213.

Schumann, J. (2010). Applied linguistics and the neurobiology of language. In R. Kaplan, (Ed.), *The Oxford handbook of applied linguistics* (pp. 244–259). Oxford: Oxford University Press.

Scollon, R. (2001) *Mediated discourse.* London: Routledge.

Tollefson, J. W. (Ed.) (2002). *Language policies in education: Critical issues.* Mahwah, NJ: Lawrence Erlbaum.

Tomasello, M. (2003). *Constructing a language.* Boston, MA: Harvard University Press.

Tomasello, M. (2008). *The origins of human communication.* Cambridge, MA: The MIT Press.

Vygotsky, L. S. (1978). *Mind in society: The development of higher psychological processes.* Cambridge, MA: Harvard University Press.

Wertsch, J. V. (1994). The primacy of mediated action in sociocultural studies. *Mind, Culture and Activity, 1,* 202–208.

Chapter 2

L2 Knowledge Is Complex and Dynamic

Overview

We all know a language. Many of us know more than one. We use our languages every day to engage in a range of social activities and accomplish a myriad of social tasks. We state our ideas, share stories, manage transactions, read reports, spend time on social media with friends, and so on. Language is so basic to our lives that we often take it for granted.

It used to be thought that the language knowledge we use to engage in our lifeworlds was an innate, self-contained, and fixed property of the human mind, a part of our genetic makeup. This property was labelled a language acquisition device and it was hypothesized that it contained a set of abstract principles, common across all languages, from which language-specific syntactic rules were generated (Chomsky, 1965). In this nativist perspective on language knowledge, social context was thought to play no role other than to trigger the activation of the device to recognize, assimilate, and articulate what was presumed to be already in our minds (Sampson, 1980).

Current understandings stand in marked contrast to the nativist view of language. They are driven by converging evidence on the nature of language and learning from several fields including child language development (e.g., Tomasello, 2001, 2003, 2006, 2008), psycholinguistics (e.g., Bates et al., 1998; Ellis 2008, 2013; Goldberg, 2003, 2006; MacWhinney, 2015), neurolinguistics (e.g., Lee et al., 2009; Schumann, 2010), and various branches of cognitive linguistics (e.g., Bowerman & Levinson, 2001; Bybee, 2006; Bybee & Noonan, 2002; Bybee & Hopper, 2001). Instead of a fixed property of human mind, language knowledge is revealed to be a complex, dynamic set of constructions that are developed from continual interaction between our neural and domain-general cognitive-emotional processes on the one hand and our varied, lifelong experiences in our social worlds on the other. These constructions are fundamentally functional; they are developed and used as means for taking action in our worlds. This understanding of language knowledge is referred to as *usage-based*. The aim of this chapter is to explore current understandings of language knowledge in more detail.

What Is Language?

A usage-based understanding considers language to be first and foremost a sociocultural resource for taking action. Through our use of language with others, we establish goals, negotiate the means to reach them, and reconceptualize those we have set. At the same time, we articulate and manage our individual identities, our interpersonal relationships, and memberships in our social groups and communities (Hall, 2011). Options for taking action in our communicative activities include a "massive collection of heterogeneous *constructions*, each with affinities to different contexts and in constant structural adaptation to usage" (Bybee & Hopper, 2001, p. 3, emphasis in the original).

Constructions

Constructions are an open set of semiotic resources "that are available to the individual in his existence as social man" (Halliday, 1973, p. 49). Semiotic resources are the material, social, and cultural means that we use to make meaning. In our use of them our constructions become conventionalized and stored in our minds as meaningful pairings of form and function that vary in terms of size and abstractness (Bybee, 2002, 2006; Bybee & Eddington, 2006; Bybee & Hopper, 2001; Ellis, 2015; Goldberg, 2003, 2006, 2013; Boyd & Goldberg, 2009; Hopper, 1998; Tomasello, 2001, 2003, 2006).

Constructions are not special units, distinguishable from what we conventionally recognize as grammar, i.e., syntactic and morphological structures. Rather, all linguistic phenomena, from very small conventional units such as morphemes and words, to phrases and clauses, along with their learned functions are constructions. In Goldberg's words, "the network of constructions captures our grammatical knowledge *in toto*, i.e. **it's constructions all the way down**" (2006, p.18, emphasis in the original). This is the case for knowledge of all languages, in all kinds of contexts (Ellis, 2008).

There is no inherent one to one correspondence between linguistic forms and functions. Linguistic forms can be used to fill many functions and functions can take many forms. Consider, for example, the English morpheme -ing. Morpheme is a conventional grammatical term used to refer to the smallest unit of meaning in a language. In this case, the form -ing is attached to verbs and, depending on the contexts of its use, serves at least three functions. First, it can be used to transform a simple verb into the progressive tense to refer to an action that is in progress, e.g., "I *am talking* to him now" and "He *was coming* from the train station".

Second, attaching -ing to a verb can transform it into an adjective that is used to describe or clarify a noun or pronoun, e.g., "The *laughing child* ran into her grandma's arms" and "Of *increasing concern* is the quality of healthcare". Third, attaching the morpheme to a simple noun transforms it into a verb to signal an action, e.g., "I'm *texting* him now" and "He's *Facebooking* his friend". Linguistic constructions can be of any size and abstractness. They range from single words such as the English items *dog*, *table*, and *planner*, connecting words such as *well*, *so*, and *anyway*, and intensifiers or emphasizers such as *really* and *totally* to groupings of words such as *inner circle* and *a round of applause*. Larger constructions include filled and partially filled multiword formulations. Examples in English can include *for all intents and purposes, give me a break, are you kidding*, and *jog (someone's) memory*. Such formulaic constructions simplify communication in that they can be "pulled directly off the mental shelf without having to build every utterance anew, from scratch" (Goldberg, 2013, p. 26).

More abstract constructions include syntactic arrangements containing, for example, verb argument structures. A common structure in English is subject-verb-object (SVO). Examples include *I ate a banana; he saw a plane; the detective solved the crime*. What we extract from use is stored not as the specific expression but, rather, the SVO pattern, with the specific lexical items used in each of the three slots varying depending on the verb and the intended meaning. The more abstract constructions are productive patterns. This means that they can be used to generate a wide range of meaningful acts. All types of constructions exist alongside each other in our minds, so that intended meanings can be potentially represented in multiple ways.

Complex Adaptive System

The constructions that comprise our individual language knowledge are not fixed grammatical systems, based on universal rules that were once latent in our minds. As Ellis (2008, p. 243) notes, "There are no mechanisms for such top-down governance". Linguistic constructions are represented in our minds as pragmatically-driven, networked collections that are learned via a complex adaptive system (Five Graces Group, 2009; Larsen-Freeman & Cameron, 2008). Pragmatically driven means that the constructions comprising our knowledge are experience based, arising as by-products from the myriad ways we organize, construe, and experience our social worlds (Goldberg, 1995; Halliday, 1973, 1978; Hymes, 1962, 1964, 1972). With our constructions, we engage and create meaning in activities with others, and through our actions, we continually work toward common ground or shared understanding of the work we are doing together (Schegloff, 2006; Tomasello, 2008).

We do not create the linguistic constructions for undertaking such work anew nor do we choose randomly from all possible constructions. Rather, our actions consist largely of conventionalized constructions whose meanings have been developed from past uses by others in similar contexts of interaction. In student–teacher interactions, for example, as teachers, we know what linguistic resources are conventionally available to us to use in our contexts of teaching and we know these from the many years we have spent as students in similar contexts, from additional years training to be teachers and from our past experiences as teachers in other contexts. It is from our engagement in these experiences, from using the options available to us to take actions and to ascribe meaning to the uses of constructions by others, that our own, communicatively significant, construction-based, language knowledge develops. From our experiences as teachers and students, for example, we have stored scores of fixed and semi-fixed formulaic constructions for use in the classroom, such as *okay, now, please open your books*, as well as *yes-no* and *wh-question* schemas, e.g., *do you/are they___, what is/who knows___*.

It is not simply through social use, however, that we come to know these constructions. Learning also entails the continual interaction of additional interdependent entities operating on different scales in time and space (Lee et al., 2009; MacWhinney, 2015; The Five Graces Group, 2009; Larsen-Freeman & Cameron, 2008; Ellis & Larsen-Freeman, 2009). As we engage in our social experiences, we make use of internal cognitive-emotional capacities such as attention, perception, memory, and motivation, of sensory systems such as the auditory and visual as well as of domain-general cognitive processes such as categorization, sequential processing, and problem solving. In addition, we make use of speech apparatuses like the teeth, tongue, and lips as well as the coordinated, and often simultaneous, use of other parts of the face and body (Macwhinney, 2015; Mondada, 2016; Schumann, 2010).

Larger entities such as social group affiliations and institutional affordances and constraints are also in play. For example, we are born into families residing in distinct geographical regions. These social group memberships make possible our engagement in particular types of schools, community organizations, and workplaces. These factors, in turn, influence the types of social activities and linguistic resources that we experience, making possible the development of some constructions over others. A simple example of this are the different words in English that are used to refer to the same object or action. Depending on where we live, some of us may learn to use the word *subway* and others *underground* to refer to the same type of public transportation. Likewise, some may learn the word *biscuit* and others *cookie* to refer to the same type of dessert or treat.

The meaningful language constructions emerging from the dynamic interactions of the various multidimensional systems are social in that they are grounded in experience and constructed in joint activities with others as we navigate our way through our interactions. They are cognitive in that they are represented in our minds as relatively automatized, functionally distributed collections of constructed patterns and practices for engaging in our social worlds.

It is important to remember that the components that emerge from the interactions of the interdependent systems do not remain static, nor is there a natural end state or complete set of constructions to be learned. Rather, the components of one's language knowledge are in a continual state of adaptation, changing as a consequence of factors ranging from individual attentional, motivational, and other dynamics to competing pragmatic intentions, changing group affiliations, and society-wide forces (Five Graces Group, 2009; Larsen-Freeman, 2006; Lee et al., 2009). Quote 2.1 summarizes the features of language as a complex adaptive system.

> **Quote 2.1 Language as a complex adaptive system**
>
> Language as a CAS [complex adaptive system] involves the following key features: The system consists of multiple agents (the speakers in the speech community) interacting with one another. The system is adaptive; that is, speakers' behavior is based on their past interactions, and current and past interactions together feed forward into future behavior. A speaker's behavior is the consequence of competing factors ranging from perceptual constraints to social motivations. The structures of language emerge from interrelated patterns of experience, social interaction, and cognitive mechanisms.
>
> The Five Graces Group (2009, pp. 1–2)

Linguist Paul Hopper (1987; Hopper & Thompson, 1993) coined the term *emergent grammar* to capture the complex, dynamic nature of language knowledge. Emergent refers to the fact that the items comprising one's knowledge are, in their use, continually being modified and are therefore unfinished and indeterminate. Hopper (1987, p. 142) offers further elaboration:

> Grammar is ... not to be understood as a prerequisite for discourse, a prior possession attributable in identical form to both speaker and hearer. Its forms are not fixed templates, but are negotiable in

face-to-face interaction in ways that reflect the individual speaker's past experience of these forms, and their assessment of the present context, including especially their interlocutors, whose experiences and assessments may be quite different.

In sum, rather than a prerequisite to individual language use, language knowledge develops from our experiences with language as we go about our daily lives. The regularities that come to define our individual language knowledge emerge from our "lifetime analysis of the distributional characteristics of the language input and their usage" (Ellis, 2006, p. 9). In other words, the constructions comprising our knowledge are individual-specific, dynamic representations that arise from our participation in constantly shifting contexts of interaction and that serve the most recurrent communicative functions in our lives. Because we are always using language, our language knowledge is in a continual state of adaptation. This is the case over the duration of our lives and no matter how many languages we know.

From Linguistic Competence to Multi-Competence

Linguistic Competence

The usage-based understanding of language has changed the way we understand the concept of *competence*, a term often used to refer to language knowledge. Its use in the SLA field can be traced back to the work of Noam Chomsky, a prominent linguist who in the 1960s proposed a theory of language in which he posited that language was a fixed, universal property of the human mind. The ability to learn language was posited to be innate and dependent on a *language acquisition device* (LAD). LAD was hypothesized to consist of a set of principles that, once triggered, generates a set of grammatical rules particular to a language. This set of rules, which "any speaker of a language knows implicitly" (Chomsky, 1966, p. 9), is what Chomsky labeled *linguistic competence.*

Communicative Competence

Dell Hymes, a renowned linguistic anthropologist and a contemporary of Chomsky, considered Chomsky's definition of linguistic competence to be inadequate in that it did not account for the social knowledge we rely on to produce and interpret utterances appropriate to the social activities in which they occur. Hymes (1964, p. 110) noted,

> it is not enough for the child to be able to produce any grammatical utterance. It would have to remain speechless if it could not decide

which grammatical utterance here and now, if it could not connect utterances to their contexts of use.

It is this social knowledge, Hymes argued, that gives meaning to linguistic forms.

He further contended that to be adequate, a theory of language must account for how "social function gives form to the ways in which linguistic features are encountered in actual life" (Hymes, 1974, p. 196). Arguing for a socially constituted linguistics, Hymes coined the term *communicative competence* to capture both the social knowledge of and ability to use linguistic resources in ways that are considered conventionally accurate and contextually appropriate within the different groups and communities to which individuals belong.

Hymes's concept of competence is distinct from Chomsky's in at least two ways. First, his term asserts a more common sense meaning of competence, by considering it to be individual ability rather than an innate, idealized system. Hymes (1972, p. 282, emphasis in the original) explained,

> I should take *competence* as the most general term for the capabilities of a person. Competence is dependent upon both (tacit) *knowledge* and (ability for) *use*...The specification of *ability for use* as part of competence allows for the role of non-cognitive factors, such as motivation, as partly determining competence.

Second, in claiming social use to be the foundation of competence, Hymes asserted the essentials of its organization to be fundamentally variable rather than universal.

Multi-Competence

By asserting a fundamental role for language use in giving shape to individual language knowledge, Hymes' concept is certainly compatible with current understandings of language knowledge as fundamentally variable, grounded in usage. In fact, Hymes' theoretical insights paved the way for decades of research on a vast range of language and literacy practices of social groups and communities around the world. The findings have revealed the rich variability in language use within and across social groups, and the links between the variable patterns of use and individuals' communicative competence.

Without denying the substantive contributions this research has made to enhancing understandings of the linguistic resources available to individuals via their social groups and communities, and differences in communicative competence *across* groups, some have noted that it has been less beneficial in uncovering the diversity of languages spoken by individuals *within* groups and the flexible skills they demonstrate in using their multiple languages. It was argued that since most individuals speak more than one language, a different concept is needed to more adequately capture the diversity of language knowledge of bilinguals and multilinguals. Hence, the term *multi-competence* was proposed, and defined as the holistic sum of multiple-language capacities (Cook, 1991, 1992, 2012; Cook & Li, 2016).

This concept has become a springboard for research on bilingual and multilingual language knowledge (Busch, 2012, 2016; Blackledge & Creese, 2010; Cook & Li, 2016; He, 2013). This research has shown how linguistically diverse the communicative resources of multilingual individuals are, and how their choices of language depend on local considerations for social action. Additional research on individual multi-competence has shown that rather than remaining stable, one's first language changes with language experiences in other languages, at all levels of linguistic constructions (Malt, Ping, Pavlenko, Zhu, & Ameel, 2015). In other words, regardless of which language one uses, the constructions comprising the multi-competence of multilingual users are in continual adaptation to usage over their lifespans.

Terms for New Understandings of Language Knowledge

Repertoires

Contemporary life in the twenty-first century has been marked by increased intensity of globalization processes, the proliferation of digital technologies along with increased internet connectivity, and sustained large-scale migration of individuals, families, and larger social groups taking place in regions around the world. People across wide geographical expanses are able to communicate daily, navigating transnational spaces via the internet, and they do so for a variety of reasons. They may communicate with family members and friends who live in faraway regions; they may take online education courses with others from different regions around the world and with different backgrounds; as consumers, they may conduct business transactions with individuals and companies across the globe. Notions of public and private domains, and social groups and affiliations are being transformed. Vertovec (2007) coined the term *super-diversity* to refer to the multidimensional processes and conditions affecting modern-day social experiences.

These varied forces and conditions have brought about profound changes to the real-world experiences of L2 learners. Along with the expansion of L2 learners' social networks, new and more varied forms of social activities are emerging. Moreover, the range of languages available to L2 learners in these activities is more numerous and the languages themselves are more hybrid or mixed (Blommaert, 2010). These ever-changing, complex super-diverse conditions and processes have given rise to new forms of semiotic resources, which, in turn, now afford or make possible new, unanticipated opportunities for the type, range, and durability of constructions that can comprise an individual's L2 knowledge.

The constructs of communicative competence and multi-competence and their presumed, inextricable links to social context notwithstanding, questions have been raised about the continued viability of the term *competence* to capture the dynamic, multilingual, and provisional composition of L2 knowledge (Blommaert, 2008; Blommaert & Backus, 2013; Busch, 2012; Canagarajah & Wurr, 2011; Hall, Cheng & Carlson, 2006; Hall, 2016; Makoni & Pennycook, 2007). Competence, it has been argued, suggests an ideology of homogeneity and permanence. And, in fact, despite the developments in research on language knowledge, many curriculum and assessment models of L2 knowledge found in schools continue to be predicated on beliefs that language knowledge is comprised of fixed, formal rules and that these rules, once learned, are not forgotten (Byrnes, 2008; Blommaert & Backus, 2011).

To counteract the implications of solidity and inflexibility that have become affiliated with the term competence, the term *repertoire* has been proposed as an alternative to refer the diversity of resources individuals learn and draw on in their social contexts of use (Blommaert & Backus, 2011; Busch, 2012; Canagarajah & Wurr, 2011; Hall, Cheng, & Carlson, 2006; Hall, 2016). John Gumperz, a linguistic anthropologist and colleague of Dell Hymes, originally defined repertoire as "the totality of linguistic resources ... available to members of particular communities" (1986, p. 20), and coined the term to refer to the variety of languages shared by groups of people in multilingual communities residing within India.

The use of the term today has become broader and, at the same time, narrower. It is broader in that it refers to a whole range of non-linguistic semiotic resources that are available to individuals for making meaning including gestures, facial expressions, and visual and other modes in addition to linguistic constructions. It is narrower in that it refers to individual knowledge of resources for communicating rather than to the resources circulating in any one community (Blommaert & Backus, 2013; Rymes, 2010; 2014).

Blommaert and Backus (2011) offer an extended discussion of the term repertoire that is supported by modern day conditions. They note that the origins of individuals' repertoires are biographical; they develop over one's lifetime through diverse "trajectories, tactics and technologies, ranging from fully formal language learning to entirely informal 'encounters' with language" (ibid., p. 1).

As the life experiences of individuals change, so do their repertoires. Depending on the trajectories of their experiences, the components of their repertoires may be more enduring. For example, constructions that are used to identify common objects and common experiences can last in one's repertoire over a lifetime. For many people, the constructions *tables*, *chairs*, and *desks* are enduring items of their repertoires as they are common to many situations, found in many contexts and used across age groups and timeframes. Other constructions are more temporary. For a few decades in the early part of the twentieth century, for example, young adults of particular social groups commonly used the multiword construction *cut a rug* to compliment someone on his or her dancing, e.g., *she really can cut a rug*. In contemporary times, the construction has fallen out of use and thus is unlikely to be found in many people's repertoires.

Other items may be in individuals' repertoires, but their strength of recollection may vary. As people age, some items associated with time periods such as childhood and teen years may disappear or stay on only as memories of past use. For example, young children in many social groups use the English terms *mama* and *dada* to address their parents. As they grow, these terms typically drop from use, and are replaced with address terms of *mom* and *dad* or *mother* and *father*.

Individual repertoires also vary by context; there are many constructions that are specific to a context, e.g., home, school, or the workplace, that may have no use outside of these contexts. As one moves from school to the workplace, for example, school-specific constructions such as *homework*, *tests*, and *teacher's pet* may be dropped from their repertoires and replaced with new constructions as individuals take on new careers and new activities. As the paths that individuals' life experiences take are not linear, neither do their repertoires develop along a straight path of ever-increasing size. Rather, they grow explosively in some stages of life, such as during early childhood, or when learning a new subject or new career, and gradually in others. All of the differences in people's life experiences will lead to the development of variable individual repertoires that are best described as "patchworks of functionally distributed communicative resources" (Blommaert & Backus, 2011, p. 9).

This understanding of language knowledge calls into question the traditional distinctions asserted to exist between monolingual and bilingual individuals. As noted previously, what gives rise to the differences in linguistic repertoires are the particular circumstances within which an individual uses language. The knowledge of individuals with more diverse social experiences, even using what is considered to be a standard language such as English or Spanish, is likely to differ from the knowledge of individuals with fewer and less diverse experiences (Canagarajah & Liyanage, 2012; Creese & Blackledge, 2015; Hall, Cheng, & Carlson, 2006).

Languaging

Alongside the arguments for the use of the term repertoire to better capture the biographical, and fundamentally variable, nature of individual language knowledge, there have been calls for new terms to refer to how individuals use their repertoires. *Languaging* is such a term (Makoni & Pennycook, 2007; Shohamy, 2006). Languaging has been defined variably as a means for L2 learners to practice, refine, and consolidate their verbal abilities in an additional language (Swain, 2006) and, more generally, as an individual's flexible use of their repertoires to take action in social contexts (Garcia & Sylvan, 2011: Creese & Blackledge, 2015). The latter definition of the term, Thibault (2011, p. 213) asserts, reminds us that language knowledge is not a "single stable state based on abstract forms", but rather, is an "open-ended meshwork of interlinked functioning components".

Translanguaging

Language use in contemporary times has softened or blurred what traditionally have been considered to be language boundaries. In shared spaces of interaction, communicating often involves the use of resources from many different languages (Blackledge & Creese, 2010; Busch, 2012; Creese & Blackledge, 2015; Garcia, 2009). Chinglish, Spanglish, and Kongish are examples of practices in which constructions from English and one or more other languages are merged in the production of utterances. Using the terms bilingual or multilingual to refer to individuals' use of such repertoires asserts a traditional view of separate languages residing in the repertoires. Such a view, it was noted earlier in the chapter, is belied by converging evidence from a range of disciplines on the fundamentally socially constructed nature of language knowledge.

To capture current usage-based understandings of language, the term *translanguaging* has been coined (Garcia, 2009; García & Li, 2014; Otheguy, Garcia, & Reid, 2015; Li, 2011). The term presumes that just one system comprises individual knowledge, containing features of various socially defined language varieties that are integrated throughout (Garcia & Li, 2014).

> **Quote 2.2 A Definition of Translanguaging**
>
> [Translanguaging is] both going between different linguistic structures and systems and going beyond them. It includes the full range of linguistic performances of multilingual language users for purposes that transcend the combination of structures, the alternation between systems, the transmission of information and the representation of values, identities and relationships. The act of translanguaging then is transformative in nature; it creates a social space for the multilingual language user by bringing together different dimensions of their personal history, experience and environment, their attitude, belief and ideology, their cognitive and physical capacity into one coordinated and meaningful performance, and making it into a lived experience.
>
> Li (2011, p. 1223)

Li Wei offers a comprehensive definition of the term in Quote 2.2 and examples of translanguaging in Quote 2.3. Li (2016) stresses that the term translanguaging is not meant as an updated term for code-switching or code-mixing (Gumperz, 1976, 1982; Myers-Scotton, 2005). These terms, like the terms bilingual and multilingual, Li and others (e.g., Canagarajah, 2013; Otheguy, Garcia & Reid, 2015) argue, are inadequate because they assume a view of language as fixed systems that exist independently from users, and suggest that "no matter how broadly and positively conceived" (Otheguy et al., 2015, p. 282), the terms still support the idea that users use separate language systems, switching between structures from each in the construction of meaning.

Translanguaging underscores the fact that meaning making is not confined to the use of languages as discrete, bounded sets of linguistic resources. Rather, the resources comprising individual repertoires are diverse and variable, and may be constructed from a number of different conventionally marked languages (Li, 2016; Otheguy, Garcia & Reid, 2015). As Canagarajah (2013, p. 41 emphasis in the original) notes,

> While the term *multilingual* perceives the relationship between languages in an additive manner (i.e., combination of separate languages), *translingual* addresses the synergy, treating languages as always in contact and mutually influencing each other, with emergent meanings and grammars.

Quote 2.3 Examples of Translanguaging

The first set of examples comes from a corpus of what I have called New Chinglish (Li, 2016a) which includes ordinary English utterances being re-appropriated with entirely different meanings for communication between Chinese users of English as well as creations of words and expressions that adhere broadly to the morphological rules of English but with Chinese twists and meanings.

1. Niubility 牛逼 = niubi, originally a taboo word, now meaning awesome ability that is worth showing off or boasting about + ability.
2. Geilivable 给力 = geili, to give force, regional dialectal expression meaning 'supportive' or 'cool' + able.
3. Chinsumer 在外疯狂购物的中国人 = a mesh of 'Chinese consumer', usually referring to Chinese tourists buying large quantities of luxury goods overseas.
4. Smilence 笑而不语 = smile + silence, referring to the stereotypical Chinese reaction of smiling without saying anything.
5. Propoorty 房地产 = describing the mounting costs property owners, especially the young.

Li (2017, pp. 3–4)

Studies by Kramsch and Whiteside (2008) and Li and Zhu (2013) are informative illustrations of translanguaging. Kramsch and Whiteside's study of negotiations between local merchants residing in a multicultural area of San Francisco, California, and speaking a variety of languages, e.g., Vietnamese, Chinese, Spanish, and English revealed that their interactions often contained a mixture of constructions from different, conventionally marked language systems. The study by Li and Zhu reveals how, in mobilizing their varied resources, a diverse group of Chinese university students living in England, and all with different histories of migration and different dialects and additional languages, created new translingual practices for taking action together. These practices, Li and Zhu conclude, show that in considering themselves to be "not Chinese from a specific place; neither are they Chinese in Britain in general. They are Chinese students at universities in London" (ibid, p. 532), the students have created new translingual spaces that underscore their fluid and dynamic identities. The translanguaging perspective of language use afforded by such studies extends our understandings of individual repertoires, making visible their mobile, adaptable, and transformative dimensions.

Summary

Converging evidence on the nature of language knowledge reveals that it is not an autonomous system, comprised of fixed sets of rules; rather, it is a "minimally sorted and organized set of memories of what people have heard and repeated over a lifetime of language use … that have arisen to serve the most recurrent functions that speakers find need to fulfil" (Ford et al., 2003: 122). These memories are emergent, dynamic, and adaptable sociocultural constructions for taking action that arise from continual interdependent interactions between our neurobiological and cognitive systems, the linguistic environments of our social worlds, and our experiences as we make meaning with others in our worlds.

As experiences vary so do individuals' language knowledge. There is no end state, then, no final stage where one's language knowledge reaches ultimate attainment. Instead, individual knowledge is always in a state of flux, with stability of one's knowledge dependent on the stability of one's experiences. Rule-like regularities, captured by linguists and documented in textbooks, are "mere descriptions, explanada not explanans" (Ellis, 2007, p. 23). In recognition of the need for terms that treat linguistic diversity as the norm and that make visible the interrelationship between what people do and what people know, terms such as repertoire and translanguaging have replaced terms such as competence and code-switching, which imply a view of languages as autonomous systems and individual knowledge as homogeneous and permanent.

Implications for Understanding L2 Teaching

A usage-based understanding of language as a complex, dynamic adaptive system opens a new door to understanding L2 teaching. Here, we lay out four implications of this understanding for L2 teaching.

1   The additional language we teach is stored and produced as constructions of various shapes and sizes that serve as sociocultural resources for taking action. It is not comprised of decontextualized grammar rules and vocabulary lists. Teaching a second language is about creating increasingly complex meaning-making contexts in which students can use their cognitive and other capabilities to expand on the repertoires they already have.

2   Language learners bring rich semiotic repertoires with them. Teaching entails developing ways to access and recruit their communicative repertoires, their experiences and their interests in meaning-making practices so that their capacities for making meaning are broadened. Learning environments should include purposeful activities that emphasize all four knowledge processes: experiencing, conceptualizing, analyzing, and applying.

3   Teaching and learning are interdependent. This means that the contexts of action we create in our classrooms have a significant effect on how and what learners learn. To restate, learners' developing repertoires are inextricably linked to their extended involvement in the regularly occurring contexts of action of our classrooms. The recurring contexts of action give fundamental shape to what individuals come to know as language and language learning.

4   L2 teaching is also about continually building your own specialized, complex, and dynamic repertoires for teaching. To expand your resources, expand the ways you teach. As the contexts of action you create in your classrooms become more complex so will your teaching repertoires.

Pedagogical Activities

The activities in this section, organized around the four types of *knowledge processes*, will assist you in relating to and making sense of the concepts that inform our understanding that *L2 knowledge is complex and dynamic*.

Experiencing

A. Language as a Complex System

Consider the following questions:

- How do current understandings of language fit with your previous understandings?
- How do current understandings reflect your language learning experiences in and out of the classroom?

Create an image that best depicts or expresses your responses to questions one and two and compare your image to those of your classmates. What conclusions can you draw from the comparisons? What implications are there for creating learning environments in your classroom with the group of students you are currently teaching or aspire to teach?

38 L2 Knowledge Is Complex and Dynamic

B. Translanguaging

Consider the following:

- How familiar are you with the practice of translanguaging?
- How well does it characterize your own language use?
- Are there specific contexts in which you usually translanguage and others in which you do not?
- What purposes do you think translanguaging serves?

After sharing your responses to these questions with others, enter *translanguaging* into an internet search engine and choose a video illustrating translanguaging in practice. After watching the video, consider the following:

- What resources are being used?
- How useful does translanguaging appear to be to its users?
- How beneficial do you think translanguaging practices would be for the learners you currently teach or aspire to teach?

Conceptualizing

A. Concept Development

Select two of the concepts listed in Box 2.1. Craft a definition of each of the two concepts in your own words. Create one or two concrete examples of the concept that you have either experienced first-hand or can imagine. Pose one or two questions that you still have about the concept and develop a way to gather more information.

Box 2.1 Concepts: L2 language knowledge is complex and dynamic

complex adaptive system	multi-competence
constructions	repertoires
communicative competence	super-diversity
linguistic competence	translanguaging

B. Concept Development

Using the internet, search for information on one of the concepts you chose above. Create a list of five or so facts about it. These can include names of

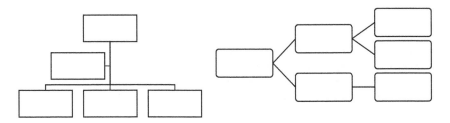

Figure 2.1 Examples of a concept web.

scholars who study the concept, studies that have been done on the concept along with their findings, visual images depicting the concept and so on. Create a concept web that visually records the information you gathered from your explorations. Figure 2.1 is an example of a concept web.

Analyzing

A. *Repertoires*

Observe a social activity that occurs frequently in your daily life. Examples include ordering a beverage in a coffee shop, chatting with friends over lunch, or checking out at a supermarket. Brainstorm other examples with your classmates. Observe several iterations of the activity over a period of time or groups of people and take field notes on the ways in which participants take action. Note the specific linguistic constructions and other semiotic resources they use for the actions. Report on the observation processes – were they easy? difficult? – and your findings to your classmates. Conclude by considering whether and how the process of analyzing the social activity expanded your own meaning-making repertoires.

B. *Translanguaging*

Dr. Ofelia Garcia, a professor at the Graduate Center of the City University of New York, is well known for her extensive work on translanguaging. In 2014, she gave a presentation on translanguaging for the National Association for Bilingual Education. You can find it here: www.youtube.com/watch?v=uk0ygruQ7pw.

Watch her presentation and take notes. After viewing the video, write a reflection paper that a. summarizes three or four main ideas presented by Professor Garcia and b. considers the promises and pitfalls of incorporating translanguaging practices in your current language classroom or one you aspire to have.

Applying

A. Repertoires

Imagine you are charged with preparing an L2 learner to successfully participate in the social activity you observed. Make a list of semiotic resources that the L2 learner might use to successfully participate in the context. Finally, create a role play or dialogue that captures two different versions for how this social activity might be accomplished. Altering the semiotic resources used will highlight variation in how this social activity can be accomplished in multiple yet meaningful ways. Finally, consider one or two ways you could recruit learners' interests and connect to their real-world experiences so that they can be successful participants in the context.

B. Language as Complex and Dynamic

Design an 8–10-minute video presentation on three to five key points discussed in this chapter for a group of pre-service teachers with little to no experience in L2 teaching. Be creative, consider using animation, visually depicting some of the concepts, incorporating clips of videos of some of the people whose works are cited in the text speaking about their topic, and even interviews with your peers on the implications of current understandings for their teaching practices. Once the video is completed, show it to your classmates for their feedback.

References

Bates, E., Elman, J., Johnson, M., Karmiloff-Smith, A., Parisi, D., & Plunkett, K. (1998). Innateness and emergentism. *A Companion to Cognitive Science*, 590–601.

Blackledge, A., & Creese, A. (2010). *Multilingualism: A critical perspective*. London: Continuum.

Blommaert, J. (2008). *Grassroots literacy: Writing, identity, and voice in Central Africa*. London: Routledge.

Blommaert, J. (2010). *The sociolinguistics of globalization*. Cambridge: Cambridge University Press.

Blommaert, J., & Backus, A. (2011). Repertoires revisited: "Knowing language" in superdiversity. *Working Papers in Urban Language & Literacies*, 67.

Blommaert, J., & Backus, A. (2013). Superdiverse repertoires and the individual. In I. De Saint-Georges & J.-J. Weber (Eds.), *Multilingualism and multimodality: Current challenges for educational studies* (pp. 11–32). Rotterdam: Sense Publishers.

Bowerman, M., & Levinson, S. C. (Eds.). (2001). *Language acquisition and conceptual development* (No. 3). Cambridge: Cambridge University Press.

Boyd, J. K., & Goldberg, A. E. (2009). Input effects within a constructionist framework. *The Modern Language Journal, 93*(3), 418–429.
Busch, B. (2012). The linguistic repertoire revisited. *Applied linguistics, 33*(5), 503–523.
Busch, B. (2016). *Categorizing languages and speakers: Why linguists should mistrust census data and statistics* (Vol. 189). Working Papers in Urban Language & Literacies.
Bybee, J. L. (2002). Consequences for the nature of constructions. In J. Bybee & M. Noonan (Eds.), *Complex sentences in grammar and discourse* (pp. 1–17). Amsterdam: John Benjamins.
Bybee, J. L. (2006). From usage to grammar: The mind's response to repetition. *Language, 82*(4), 711–733.
Bybee, J. L., & Eddington, D. (2006). A usage-based approach to Spanish verbs of "becoming". *Language, 82*(2), 323–355.
Bybee, J., & Hopper, P. (2001) Introduction to frequency and the emergence of linguistic structure. In J. Bybee & P. Hopper (Eds.), *Frequency and the emergence of linguistic structure* (pp. 1–24). Amsterdam: John Benjamins.
Bybee, J. L., & Noonan, M. (Eds.) (2002). *Complex sentences in grammar and discourse: Essays in honor of Sandra A. Thompson*. Amsterdam: John Benjamins Publishing.
Byrnes, H. (2008). *Advanced language learning: The contribution of Halliday and Vygotsky*. London: Continuum.
Canagarajah, A. S. (2013). Negotiating translingual literacy: An enactment. *Research in the Teaching of English*, 40–67.
Canagarajah, A. S., & Wurr, A. J. (2011). Multilingual communication and language acquisition: New research directions. *The Reading Matrix, 11*(1), 1–15.
Canagarajah, A. S., & Liyanage, I. (2012). Lessons from pre-colonial multilingualism. In M. Martin-Jones, A. Blackledge & A. Creese (Eds.), *Routledge handbook of multilingualism* (pp. 49–65). London: Routledge.
Chomsky, N. (1965). *Aspects of a theory of syntax*. Cambridge, MA: MIT Press.
Chomsky, N. (1966). *Topics in the theory of generative grammar*. The Hague: Mouton.
Cook, V. (1991). The poverty-of-the-stimulus argument and multicompetence. *Second Language Research 7*, 103–117.
Cook, V. (1992). Evidence for multicompetence. *Language Learning, 42*(4), 557–591.
Cook, V. (2012). Multi-competence. In C. Chapelle (Ed.), *The encyclopedia of applied linguistics* (pp. 3768–3774). New York: Wiley-Blackwell.
Cook, V., & Li, W. (Eds.) (2016). *The Cambridge handbook of linguistic multi-competence*. Cambridge: Cambridge University Press.
Creese, A., & Blackledge, A. (2015). Translanguaging and identity in educational settings. *Annual Review of Applied Linguistics, 35*, 20–35.
Ellis, N. C. (2006). Language acquisition as rational contingency learning. *Applied linguistics, 27*(1), 1–24.
Ellis, N. C. (2007). Dynamic systems theory and SLA: The wood and the trees. *Bilingualism: Language and Cognition, 10*(1), 23–25.

Ellis, N. C. (2008). The dynamics of second language emergence: Cycles of language use, language change, and language acquisition. *The Modern Language Journal*, 92(2), 232–249.

Ellis, N. C. (2013). Emergentism. In C. Chapelle (Ed.), *The encyclopedia of applied linguistics*. New York: Wiley-Blackwell.

Ellis, N. C. (2015). Implicit *and* explicit learning: Their dynamic interface and complexity. In P. Rebuschat (Ed.), *Implicit and explicit learning of languages* (pp. 3–23). Amsterdam: John Benjamins.

Ellis, N. C., & Larsen-Freeman, D. (2009). *Language as a complex adaptive system* (Vol. 3). John Wiley & Sons.

The Five Graces Group (Beckner, C., Blythe, R., Bybee, J., Christiansen, M. H., Croft, W., Ellis, N.C., Holland, J. Ke, J., Larsen-Freeman, D., Schoenemann, T.) (2009). Language is a complex adaptive system. Position paper, Language Learning, 59, Supplement 1, 1–17.

Ford, C. E., Fox, B. A., & Thompson, S. A. (2003). Social interaction and grammar. *The new psychology of language*, 2, 119–143.

García, O. (2009). *Bilingual education in the 21st century*. Oxford: Blackwell.

García, O., & Li, W. (2014). *Translanguaging: Language, education, and bilingualism*. New York: Palgrave Macmillan.

García, O., & Sylvan, C. E. (2011). Pedagogies and practices in multilingual classrooms: Singularities in pluralities. *The Modern Language Journal*, 95(3), 385–400.

Goldberg, A. E. (1995). *Constructions: A construction grammar approach to argument structure*. Chicago: University of Chicago Press.

Goldberg, A. E. (2003). Constructions: a new theoretical approach to language. *Trends in Cognitive Sciences*, 7(5), 219–224.

Goldberg, A. E. (2006). *Constructions at work: The nature of generalization in language*. Oxford: Oxford University Press.

Goldberg, A. E. (2013). Constructionist approaches. In T. Hoffmann & G. Trousdale (Eds.), *The Oxford handbook of construction grammar* (pp. 15–31). Oxford: Oxford University Press.

Group, T. F. G. (2009). Language is a complex adaptive system: Position paper. *Language Learning*, 59(s1), 1–26.

Gumperz, J. (1972/1986). Introduction. In J. Gumperz, & D. Hymes (Eds.), *Directions in sociolinguistics: The ethnography of communication* (pp. 1–25). London: Blackwell.

Gumperz, J. J. (1976). *Social network and language shift*. California: University of California Press.

Gumperz, J. J. (1982). *Discourse strategies*. Cambridge: Cambridge University Press.

Hall, J. K. (2011). *Teaching and researching language and culture*, 2nd ed. London: Pearson.

Hall, J. K. (2016) A usage-based view of multicompetence. In V. Cook & W. Li (Eds.), *Cambridge handbook of linguistic multi-competence* (pp. 183–206) Cambridge: Cambridge University Press.

Hall, J. K., Cheng, A., & Carlson, M. (2006). Reconceptualizing multicompetence as a theory of language knowledge. *Applied Linguistics*, 27(2), 220–240.

Halliday, M. A. K. (1973). *Explorations in the functions of language*. London: Edward Arnold.

Halliday, M. A. K. (1978). *Language as social semiotic* (p. 136). London: Edward Arnold.
Hopper, P. (1987). Emergent grammar. *Berkeley Linguistics Society, 13*, 139–157.
Hopper, P. (1998). Emergent grammar. In M. Tomasello (Ed.), *New psychology of language* (pp. 155–175). Mahwah, NJ: Erlbaum.
Hopper, P., & Thompson, S. (1993). Language universals, discourse pragmatics and semantics. *Language Sciences, 15*, 357–376.
Hymes, D. (1962). The ethnography of speaking. In T. Gladwin & W. Sturtevant (Eds.), *Anthropology and human behavior* (pp. 15–53). Washington, DC: Anthropological Society of Washington.
Hymes, D. (1964). Formal discussion. *The acquisition of language: Monographs of the society for research in child development, 29*, 107–111.
Hymes, D. (1972). On communicative competence. In J. B. Pride & J. Holmes (Eds.), *Sociolinguistics* (pp. 269–293). Harmondsworth: Penguin.
Hymes, D. (1974) *Foundations in sociolinguistics: An ethnographic approach.* Philadelphia: University of Pennsylvania Press.
Kramsch, C., & Whiteside, A. (2008). Language ecology in multilingual settings. Towards a theory of symbolic competence. *Applied Linguistics, 29*(4), 645–671.
Larsen-Freeman, D. (2006). The emergence of complexity, fluency, and accuracy in the oral and written production of five Chinese learners of English. *Applied Linguistics, 27*(4), 590–619.
Larsen-Freeman, D., & Cameron, L. (2008). *Complex systems and applied linguistics.* New York: Oxford University Press.
Lee, N., Mikesell, L., Joaquin, A. D. L., Mates, A. W., & Schumann, J. H. (2009). *The interactional instinct: The evolution and acquisition of language.* New York: Oxford University Press.
Li, W. (2011). Moment analysis and translanguaging space: Discursive construction of identities by multilingual Chinese youth in Britain. *Journal of Pragmatics, 43*, 1222–1235.
Li, W. (2016). New Chinglish and the post-multilingualism challenge: Translanguaging ELF in China. *Journal of English as a Lingua Franca, 5*(1), 1–25.
Li, W. (2017). Translanguaging as a practical theory of language. *Applied Linguistics, 39*(1), 9–30.
Li, W., & Zhu, H. (2013). Translanguaging identities and ideologies: Creating transnational space through flexible multilingual practices amongst Chinese university students in the UK. *Applied Linguistics, 34*(5), 516–535.
MacWhinney, B. (2015). Multidimensional SLA. In T. Cadierno & S. Eskildsen (Eds.), *Usage-based perspectives on second language learning* (pp. 22–45). Berlin: DeGruyter.
Makoni, S., & Pennycook, A. (Eds.) (2007). *Disinventing and reinventing languages.* Clevedon: Multilingual Matters.
Malt, B. C., Li, P., Pavlenko, A., Zhu, H., & Ameel, E. (2015). Bidirectional lexical interaction in late immersed Mandarin-English bilinguals. *Journal of Memory and Language, 82*, 86–104.
Mondada, L. (2016). Challenges of multimodality: Language and the body in social interaction. *Journal of Sociolinguistics, 20*(3), 336–366.
Myers-Scotton, C. (2005). *Multiple voices: An introduction to bilingualism.* Wiley-Blackwell.

Otheguy, R., García, O., & Reid, W. (2015). Clarifying translanguaging and deconstructing named languages: A perspective from linguistics. *Applied Linguistics Review*, 6(3), 281–307.

Rymes, B. (2010). Classroom discourse analysis: A focus on communicative repertoires. In N. Hornberger & S. McKay (Eds.), *Sociolinguistics and language education* (pp. 528–546). Clevedon: Multilingual Matters.

Rymes, B. (2014). Communicative repertoire. In B. Street & C. Leung (Eds.), *The Routledge companion to English studies*. London: Routledge.

Sampson, G. (1980). *Schools of linguistics*. Stanford, CA: Stanford University Press.

Schegloff, E. A. (2006). Interaction: The infrastructure for social institutions, the natural ecological niche for language, and the arena in which culture is enacted. In N. Enfield & S. Levinson (Eds.), *Roots of human sociality: Culture, cognition and interaction* (pp. 70–96). New York: Berg.

Schumann, J. (2010). Applied linguistics and the neurobiology of language. In R. Kaplan (Ed.), *The Oxford handbook of applied linguistics*, 2nd edition (pp. 244–259). Oxford: Oxford University Press.

Shohamy, E. (2006). *Language policy: Hidden agendas and new approaches*. London: Routledge.

Swain, M. (2006). Languaging, agency and collaboration in advanced second language learning. In H. Byrnes (Ed.), *Advanced language learning: The contribution of Halliday and Vygotsky* (pp. 95–108). London: Continuum.

Thibault, P. J. (2011). First-order languaging dynamics and second-order language: The distributed language view. *Ecological Psychology*, 23(3), 210–245.

Tomasello, M. (2001). Perceiving intentions and learning words in the second year of life. In M. Bowerman & S. Levinson (Eds.), *Language acquisition and conceptual development* (pp. 132–158). Cambridge: Cambridge University Press.

Tomasello, M. (2003). *Constructing a language: A usage-based theory of language acquisition*. Cambridge, MA: Harvard University Press.

Tomasello, M. (2006). Acquiring linguistic constructions. In R. S. Siegler & D. Kuhn (Eds.), *Handbook of child psychology: Cognitive development* (pp. 255–298). New York: Wiley.

Tomasello, M. (2008). *Origins of human cognition*. Cambridge, MA: MIT Press.

Vertovec, S. (2007). Super-diversity and its implications. *Ethnic and Racial Studies*, 30, 1024–1054.

Weiyun He, A. (2013). The Wor(l)d is a collage: multi-performance by Chinese heritage language speakers. *The Modern Language Journal*, 97(2), 304–317.

Chapter 3

L2 Knowledge Is a Repertoire of Diverse Semiotic Resources

Overview

By and large studies of L2 learning have focused on learners' development of conventional linguistic units such as vocabulary words and grammar or syntactic rules. However, we know that making meaning involves far more than words. Linguistic constructions are only one set of the many resources available to us in our activities for making and interpreting meaning. Nonverbal behaviors, for example, play a significant role in communication. We may point or gesture as we speak to indicate something or to emphasize a point. We also use eye gaze and facial expressions to communicate. Smiling when speaking or when listening to someone else speak can convey an affiliative stance toward the topic of the interaction or the persons with whom we are interacting. Technologies such as tablets, smart phones, and the internet have also broadened the scope of resources we use to interpret and make meaning. Images and graphic symbols such as pictographs and emojis have become common resources for representing a wide range of objects, places, people, emotions, and even ideas and concepts. All of the various means we use to communicate are called semiotic resources. In this chapter, we examine more closely the various semiotic resources that are available to us for making and interpreting meaning in our social worlds.

What Are Semiotic Resources?

As discussed in Chapter 2, our individual language knowledge is comprised of a wide range of linguistic constructions, stored in our minds as form-meaning pairings, that we develop and use in the myriad activities we engage in daily in our social worlds. It is not just with words, however, that we make meaning. In addition to language, we draw on a wide array of other means to make and interpret meaning in contexts of interaction. The term *semiotic resources* is used to refer to all of the various means of making meaning.

As shown in Figure 3.1, in addition to linguistic constructions, semiotic resources include prosodic conventions such as intonation, stress, tempo, pausing, and other features that accompany speech. Our semiotic resources also include nonverbal means of meaning making such as facial expressions, eye gaze, gesture, body positionings, and movement. For example, smiling, frowning, furrowing our brows, raising our hands, and pointing, either with speech or alone, can all perform different actions. In the case of writing, in addition to conventional linguistic constructions, semiotic resources include typescript, punctuation, and other typographic and orthographic conventions. Additional resources include graphic and pictorial modes such as diagrams, maps, and pictures, and artifactual modes such as objects, writing implements, and electronic devices. In fact, semiotic resources can be anything that is used with a communicative purpose.

Multimodality

Each type of semiotic resource is a socially made and culturally available *mode* for making meaning (Kress, 2014). A mode is a "regularised organised set of resources for meaning-making, including, image, gaze, gesture, movement, music, speech and sound-effect" (Jewitt & Kress, 2003, p. 1). The term *multimodality* refers to the multiplicity of modes in

ARTIFACTUAL • objects • materials	NONVERBAL • facial expressions • gazes • body positionings
AUDIO • music • ambient sounds	ORTHOGRAPHIC • typescript • punctuation
GRAPHIC • diagrams • maps • illustrations	PICTORIAL • images • emojis
INTERACTIONAL • actions • turn taking • routines	PROSODIC • rhythm • pitch • emphasis
LINGUISTIC • words • collocations of words	SPATIAL • layout • proximity

Figure 3.1 Examples of semiotic resources.

addition to speech and writing that individuals mobilize to make meaning. The term draws attention to the fact that human actions are built through the combination of many meaning-making modes at one time.

Spoken words, for example, are always accompanied by prosodic conventions such as intonation and stress. Varying these qualities can create different actions (Ochs, 1996). For example, varying the qualities of emphasis and intonation when uttering the word "hey" in English, changes the action being performed. Depending on how it is spoken, it can be a greeting, an attention getter, or even or an admonition. Moreover, spoken words are typically accompanied by particular arrangements of facial expressions, gestures such as head nods, and body movements. For example, to indicate a shared point of reference as we speak we may point with a finger or head tilt. Our words can also be accompanied by hand movements that, for example, hold an object such as a sign, or touch the screen of a smart pad.

Written text is also multimodal. Words in a text are rendered with particular visual dimensions such as font styles, sizes, and colors, and with particular page styles and spatial designs (Kress, 2010). The different assemblages or arrangements of resources serve different purposes. Depending on the visual and spatial arrangements of words on a page, the text might serve as an advertisement, a news headline, or an invitation. Depending on the material on which the words appear, e.g., a large outdoor board or a concrete wall, the text may be interpreted as a commercial sign or an expression of art.

The concept of a *multimodal ensemble* refers to the combination of modes in the making of meaning. It draws attention to the integration of a plurality of modes in the production and interpretation of actions (Goodwin, 2003; Jewitt, 2008; Kress, 2010; Mondada, 2016). The following two examples demonstrate how intertwined different modes are in performing actions. Consider a cooking show that airs on television. Observing what the chef is doing while she is speaking reveals how her actions are built through the juxtaposition of several modes. She may be holding a measuring cup in one hand, and, as she speaks, she may simultaneously pour what is in the cup into a bowl that she is touching with her other hand, moving her gaze between the camera and the bowl.

As another example, consider the synchronized use of multiple modes in addition to language that is entailed in teaching. Teachers must calibrate their language, facial expressions, gestures, body positions, and even the use of material artifacts such as a textbook or smart pad such that the pedagogical project is advanced, the shared attention of students is maintained, and individual student participation is promoted. Even allocating turns at talk occasions the synchronized use of eye gaze, head nods, and finger pointing (Kääntä, 2012; Mortensen, 2009).

These examples make clear that taking action, i.e., making meaning, involves complex ensembles of various semiotic modes, with language being but one of them (Early, Kendrick, & Potts, 2015; Goodwin, 2003; Kress, 2010). As Goodwin (2003, pp. 22–23) notes, "rather than being lodged in a single modality... many forms of human action are built through the juxtaposition of quite diverse materials, including the actor's body, the bodies of others, language, structure in the environment, and so on". In fact, in most cases, the actions that individuals build for each other in their social activities cannot be located in any single mode (Streeck, Goodwin, & LeBaron, 2011).

Meaning potentials

All semiotic resources, individually and in combination, have *meaning potentials*, i.e., conventionalized meanings that develop from their uses. Their conventionalized meanings represent the ways that groups and communities in the past have used the resources to accomplish particular goals that, in turn, are shaped by larger social institutions, e.g., the family, schools, communities, etc. and larger cultural and historical forces.

Meaning potentials of semiotic resources are not universal; they are context-sensitive with particular meanings activated or motivated by the contexts in which they appear. One implication of this is that the meaning of a resource in one context can be different when used in a different context. Take the English address term "ma'am", for example. In some communities in the southern regions of the United States, it is considered a marker of politeness and respect and is used to by young people whenever they address their female elders. Not doing so is considered a sign of disrespect. In contrast, in communities in the northern regions of the United States, the use of ma'am for addressing adult women is considered by some to be old-fashioned, and even offensive to women. Using it to address a woman would be considered rude. In Quote 3.1, Mikhail Bakhtin, a renowned Russian philosopher of language, explains the historical relationship that exists between language and meaning.

Quote 3.1 The Relation Between Language Use and Meaning

There are no 'neutral' words and forms – words and forms that belong to 'no one'; language has been completely taken over, shot through with intentions and actions. For any individual consciousness living in it, language is not an abstract system of normative forms but rather a concrete heterglot conception of the world. All

> words have the 'taste of a profession, a genre, a tendency, a party, a particular work, a particular person, a generation, an age group, the day and hour. Each word tastes of the context and contexts in which it has lived its socially charged life; all words and forms are populated by intentions.
>
> Bakhtin (1981, p. 293)

The meaning potentials of all semiotic resources are considered *affordances* in that in their local contexts of use, they offer particular visions of the world, that is, different possibilities for action, and different interpretive possibilities (Byrnes, 2006; Hall, 2011). For example, consider a greeting between two English speaking professionals, one a man and the other a woman. There is an array of conventional linguistic resources that they can choose for taking such actions, including *"hi"*, *"hello, how are you"*, *"good day"*, *"hey, babe"*, *"wussup"*, *"yo"*, and *"what it be"*, among many others. Each of these resources has a history of meaning that calls to mind particular contexts of use by particular individuals with particular communicative goals. Their use affords, i.e., makes possible, particular meanings and interpretations of experiences. The specific greeting the two professionals choose to use will construe their experience differently, from very informal to very formal and their relationship from close, perhaps even intimate friends, to neighbors, or to colleagues. Tomasello (1999, p. 8) provides another example on how the same object, event, or place can be construed differently by the use of different words depending individual communicative goals:

> in different communicative situations one and the same object may be construed as a dog, an animal, a pet, or a pest; one and the same event may be construed as running, moving, fleeing, or surviving; one and the same place may be construed as the coast, the shore, the beach, or the sand – all depending on the communicative goals of the speaker.

Nonverbal behaviors likewise have different meaning potentials. The same resource can present different meanings depending on the context. For example, a raised hand can signal that one wants a turn to speak or to stop an action, or that someone is taking an oath in a courtroom prior to offering testimony. Conversely, similar actions can be enacted with different nonverbal resources. We can attempt to stop someone from doing something by a shake of the head, a raised hand with the palm facing outward, or by an extended gaze with furrowed brow, with choices for the type of resource used determined by the particular context of interaction and the communicative goal of the individual in that context.

Objects, too, have different meaning potentials. For example, maps represent particular characteristics and locations of places, making it possible for users to navigate from one place to another. Calendars order days into time periods making it possible for users to organize and remember events. Public road signs inform, warn, and redirect drivers and pedestrians as they travel from one place to another.

The term *modal affordance* refers to "the material and the cultural aspects of modes: what it is possible to express and represent easily with a mode" (Jewitt, 2013, p. 149). No one mode is considered essential to meaning making. Rather, each contributes to the construction of meaning in different ways. To state another way, each semiotic mode offers particular possibilities for expression and representation. For example, the production of speech relies on articulators such as the tongue, lips, and other speech organs. Articulated constructions are produced in real time; each follows another, in sequential order. These are some of the affordances of the mode of speech. It is impossible, however, to verbally produce more than one construction at a time. This is one of the constraints of speech.

The affordances of images differ from speech in at least two ways. First, individuals rely on graphic or photo design tools rather than on speech articulators to produce meaning and second, since meaning is represented spatially, they afford the simultaneous representation of different meanings. For instance, viewing an image of a group of people, each engaged in a different activity, affords different understandings of the meanings enacted in the image than does listening to or reading a narrative describing the image.

Even spatial arrangements of objects such as tables and chairs afford different meaning-making potentials. In learning spaces like classrooms, for example, desks and chairs are key resources. Figure 3.2 displays some of the many ways that classroom spaces can be configured. Each possibility offers, i.e., affords, different types of instructional activities, different interactions between teachers and students, different opportunities for access to materials such as electronic devices and so on.

The pictures in Figure 3.2 display different classroom seating arrangements. In picture (a), we see that the desks are arranged in groups of three or four. This arrangement makes possible small group work and allows the teacher to freely circulate among the groups and interact with individuals and groups of students. In addition, the desks are not affixed to the floor, which allows them to be reconfigured by the teacher and students to make possible other kinds of learning activities. Picture (b) is quite different. It depicts a hall with theater seating, the arrangement of which readily affords teacher-fronted lessons such as

Figure 3.2 Semiotic resources of classrooms.

lectures or demonstrations. However, while the arrangement of the seats allows students full visual access to the instructor, it limits the kind of instructional activities that can occur. It also limits the amount and type of interaction that can occur between the instructor and students and movement of the instructor among the students.

In picture (c), we can see that while the space is smaller than that in picture two, the arrangement of desks and chairs is somewhat similar in that the desks are in rows, facing the front of the room. This arrangement allows for teacher-fronted lessons and affords students visual access to the teacher but it constrains the teacher's access to individual students and the types of learning activities that can occur. In picture (d), we can see that seating is organized quite differently. There are several tables in the room on which sit computers and for each computer there is a chair. Such an arrangement easily affords individual instruction, facilitated by the electronic device each student faces. In all cases, there is no seating arrangement that is better than another. Rather, each affords particular teaching and learning opportunities.

As noted previously, the affordances of our semiotic resources develop from their past uses. Their histories of use become their "provenance, shaping available designs and uses" (Jewitt, 2008, p. 247). While the resources' conventionalized meanings bind individuals to some degree to particular ways of making meaning with them, how they come to mean at a particular communicative moment, i.e., the personalized meaning potentials that individuals are able to create, is always open to negotiation (Mattiessen, 2009). In their uses of their resources at a particular moment in a particular context, individuals choose "a particular way of entering the world and a particular way of sustaining relationships with others" (Duranti, 1997, p. 46). The term *design* was coined by the New London Group (1996, 2000) to capture the dynamic processes by which individuals make meaning with their available resources. To design is to create meanings through the organization of semiotic resources in ways to achieve one's communicative purposes (Cope & Kalantzis, 2009; Kress, 2010, 2014).

Communicative Repertoires

The term repertoire was introduced in Chapter 2 to refer to the totality of linguistic constructions that we develop in our life experiences. Here, we expand the term to include all of the meaning-making resources that we use to participate in the multiple communities to which we belong (Rymes, 2010). The term *communicative* emphasizes not only the functional nature of the resources comprising our repertoires but their diversity as well.

The resources comprising our repertoires do not exist in random relation to each other. Rather, they are linked to *registers* and *schemas of expectations* for their use. Registers comprise sets of semiotic resources that, in their use, are associated with particular activities, particular institutional contexts, and with particular people who engage in such activities and contexts (Agha, 2004). They can vary in terms of degree of formality of resources used to make meaning. For example, we have registers that are associated with school, home, commercial businesses, and professions such as medicine, the law, and teaching. Registers are also associated with particular social roles, such as parents, teachers, students, doctors, lawyers, judges, and so on. Schemas of expectations are ethnographically-grounded understandings, "sedimented social knowledge" (Hanks, 1996, p. 238) that individuals have about the contexts to which their resources and registers are connected and how they function in their social works (Levinson, 2006).

Box 3.1 is an example of how schemas of expectations of resource meanings are exploited to humorous effect. This was found on a sign outside of a church located in the southern region of the United States. For many social groups, the English utterance "Don't make me come down there" evokes the social roles of parents and children, and a typical situation in which one or some children are misbehaving.

> **Box 3.1 On a sign outside of a church**
>
> Don't make me have to come down there
>
> —God

Stated by the parent, the utterance serves to reprimand the children for their behavior. While the consequences for ignoring the warning are not stated, it is implied that they will be dire if the actions do not stop. Attributing the utterance to God, believed by many to be the supreme protector of all humanity, suggests a similar context of use. In this case, the utterance ascribes to God the role of reproaching parent to a world filled with badly behaved children.

As the paths that our life experiences take are not linear, neither do the registers comprising our communicative repertoires develop along a straight path of ever-increasing size. Rather, they arise from a "wide variety of trajectories, tactics and technologies, ranging from fully formal language learning to entirely informal 'encounters' with language" (Blommaert & Backus, 2012, p. 1). As we meet new people, take on new goals, enter into new activities or new institutions or move to new communities, some of our resources may become more entrenched or well-established, others may change, others forgotten and still others may simply disappear.

Super-Diverse Communicative Repertoires

The world is ever more complex. Large scale migration within and across regions, nations, and continents continues to bring people from around the world together in groups, communities, schools, workplaces, places of worship, and other social institutions. People come with highly varied nationalities, ethnicities, languages, and life experiences and as a result of widely varying motives for moving that range from conflict, war and famine, to educational advancement, economic aspirations, and global business.

Adding to the complexity is the continued advancement of information technologies and social networking sites that bring people from diverse geographical locations around the world together to exchange information, share interests, and develop, maintain, and extend social relationships. Together, these forces have not only afforded the wide and rapid circulation of semiotic resources across individuals, groups, and communities, but they have also given rise to new, complex, multilingual, and multimodal semiotic resources (Rymes, 2012; Blommaert, 2013). Blommaert (2012, p. 13) explains, "in superdiverse environments (both on- and offline), people appear to take any linguistic and communicative resource available to them ... and blend them into hugely complex linguistic and semiotic forms". The value of the term communicative repertoire in capturing the impact of these super-diverse forces on individuals' semiotic resources is this:

> Repertoires enable us to document in great detail the trajectories followed by people throughout their lives: the opportunities, constraints and inequalities they were facing, the learning environments they had access to (and those they did not have access to), their movement across physical and social space, their potential for voice in particular social arenas.
> (Blommaert & Backus, 2011, p. 24)

Summary

The resources at our disposal for making meaning involve more than just language. They include complex ensembles of various semiotic modes for making and interpreting meaning. The histories of meanings attached to our semiotic resources afford us particular ways of construing our worlds. We use them to design meanings in particular contexts of use to achieve our communicative purposes. The many meaning-making resources we use to participate in our social worlds comprise our communicative repertoires. Our repertoires are not locked, impermeable to change, but are massively dynamic, responsive to conditions at all levels of social activity. As our life experiences in our social worlds change, so do the resources comprising our repertoires. All else being equal, the greater the diversity of experiences we have, linguistically and otherwise, the more diverse our repertoires are.

Implications for Understanding L2 Teaching

Language is at the heart of language teaching. Understanding what language is affects how we teach. Three implications for understanding L2 teaching can be derived from an understanding of language knowledge as repertoires of diverse semiotic resources.

1   Understanding language knowledge as repertoires of diverse semiotic resources changes how we understand the activity of teaching. Making and interpreting meaning in contexts of action involve not just linguistic constructions, but a plurality of modes. This is the case for teaching *and* learning, in fact, for *any* kind of social activity. Imagine reducing the activity of teaching to just one mode. It

is impossible. We cannot speak without using prosodic cues such as stress and rhythm. We cannot write without choosing a writing system and deciding whether to type or write by hand. We cannot teach without deciding on a type of spatial arrangement. Contributing to the work of teaching are artifacts, often used simultaneously with talk, and gestures and other body movements that serve to secure and maintain learners' attention as we speak. It is a fact that teaching cannot be accomplished without utilizing a number of multimodal ensembles. Focusing attention on only one mode renders invisible the complex and specialized multimodal work of teaching.

2 Understanding language knowledge as repertoires of diverse semiotic resources also changes how we understand the objects of L2 learning. Learning another language is about much more than just learning *language*, e.g., conventionally prescribed grammar rules. Privileging language as the central, only means of full expression and representation is inadequate for meeting the challenges of living in contemporary times. Rather than constraining learners' choices for meaning making, we need to expand opportunities for learners to adopt new resources and new ways of using already familiar resources so that their multilingual and multimodal options enable them to bring their social worlds into existence, maintain them, and transform them for their own purposes. The *what* they learn is conceived not only as structures of resources. Rather, it is also, and more importantly, conceived as ways of designing. L2 learning then is about learning how to choose from the vast range of available resources to (re)create learners' potential in ways that project their "interest into their world with the intent of effect in the future" (Kress, 2010, p. 23).

3 Our learners live in an ever-changing world. Every day they come into contact with new people, new contexts of action, and new meaning-making resources. Their meaning-making skills reach far beyond what we can imagine. Rather than treating their skills and knowledge as peripheral to the work we do in our classrooms, we must embrace them, that is, "recruit ... the different subjectivities, interests, intentions, commitments and purposes that students bring to learning" (The New London Group, 2000, p.18), and use them to inform our classroom practices.

Pedagogical Activities

The activities in this section, organized around the four types of *knowledge processes*, will assist you in relating to and making sense of the concepts that inform our understanding that *L2 knowledge comprises repertoires of diverse semiotic resources.*

Experiencing

A. Semiotic Resources

Watch this commercial from Sheraton Hotels and Resorts in which the narrator states: "The greetings are different, the need to feel welcome is the same. You don't just stay here, you belong."
www.youtube.com/watch?v=03WjUebwc2s
After watching the commercial a few times, consider the following:

- What are two different types of greetings shown in the video and what semiotic resources are used in each?
- How similar or different are they in terms of the semiotic resources that are used?
- How similar or different are they to the various ways in which people from your social group(s) greet one another?
- What implications can you draw from your findings for L2 teaching?

B. Semiotic Resources

Take or find two or three photos of different types of classrooms and address the following questions individually or in small groups.

- What semiotic resources are in each of the rooms?
- What are the meaning potentials of each resource?
- What kinds of experiences have you had in each type?
- How do you think the resources and spatial arrangements that you are familiar with have influenced the ways you learn? The ways you have taught or will teach?
- What conclusions can you draw about how the designs of learning environments shape L2 teaching and learning?

Conceptualizing

A. Concept Development

Select two of the concepts listed in Box 3.2. Craft a definition of each of the two concepts in your own words. Create one or two concrete examples of the concept that you have either experienced first-hand or can imagine. Pose one or two questions that you still have about the concept and develop a way to gather more information.

> **Box 3.2 Concepts: L2 knowledge is a repertoire of diverse semiotic resources**
>
> design
> communicative repertoire
> meaning potentials
> modal affordance
>
> mode
> multimodality
> multimodal ensemble
> semiotic resource

B. Communicative Repertoires

Read the quote by Christian Matthiessen and restate in your own words. Design a multimodal text that captures the substance of your understanding. The text can be paper (e.g., written text such as a personal narrative or poster that incorporates images or graphics) or digital (e.g., a video or slide presentation that incorporates written and/or spoken language, images, sound). Together with your class, decide on how to make your work publically available to others.

> When people learn languages, they build up their own personalized meaning potentials as part of the collective meaning potential that constitutes the language, and they build up these personal potentials by gradually expanding their own registerial repertoires—their own shares in the collective meaning potential. As they expand their own registerial repertoires, they can take on roles in a growing range of contexts, becoming semiotically more empowered and versatile.
>
> (2009, p. 223)

Analyzing

A. Meaning Potentials

Explore the *positive lexicography project*, developed by Tim Lomas, a lecturer at the University of East London. The project is an evolving index of "'untranslatable' words related to wellbeing from across the world's languages". According to its developer, the project aims to highlight different constructions by which cultures express well-being.

You can find the project at this site: www.drtimlomas.com/lexicography.

On the home page, click on the link *Interactive lexicography* and choose a theme to explore. Explain the findings from your explorations in terms of the meaning potentials and then consider the following question:

- What implications for understanding the concept of meaning potentials can you derive from this project and from your explorations?

B. Multimodality

Head to this site on multimodality and learning: http://inclusiveclassrooms.org/practice/multimodality

The site is part of the Teachers College Inclusive Classroom Project (TCICP), which supports the development of educational practices that focus on inclusion in their classrooms. At the site, choose one or two of the projects to explore. In your explorations, take note of how multimodal resources are integrated into the projects and how useful the teachers found the projects to be to their own learning. Finally, consider the following question:

- What implications about the value of multimodality can you derive for your own learning and for your L2 teaching context?

Applying

A. Multimodality

Using what you learned from your explorations at the TCICP site on multimodality, individually or collaboratively, create a digital multimodal story. The topic should be broadly related to L2 teaching and learning. There are many resources on the internet to help you. Type *digital storytelling* into an internet browser to locate them. Once completed, decide with your classmates on ways to disseminate your stories to a wider audience.

B. Multimodality

Using what you learned from the experience of creating your own story, individually or collaboratively, design a lesson on digital storytelling for a specific group of L2 learners. Before you begin, gather ideas from others. One easy way to do this is to type *digital storytelling for L2 learners* in an internet browser. Share what you find with your classmates and, together, decide on a set of components to include in the lesson. Once your lesson is completed, present it to your classmates. If possible, share lessons by uploading them to a public folder on the network.

References

Agha, A. (2004). Registers of language. In A. Duranti (Ed.), *A companion to linguistic anthropology* (pp. 23–45). Oxford: Blackwell.

Bakhtin, M. M. (1981). *The dialogic imagination* (Ed. M. Holquist). Austin: University of Texas Press.

Blommaert, J. (2012). Chronicles of complexity: Ethnography, superdiversity, and linguistic landscapes. *Tilburg Papers in Culture Studies*, 29, 1–149.

Blommaert, J. (2013). Citizenship, language, and superdiversity: Towards complexity. *Journal of Language, Identity, and Education*, 12, 193–196.
Blommaert, J., & Backus, A. (2012). Superdiverse repertoires and the individual. In I. de Saint-Georges and J. Weber (Eds.), *Multilingualism and multimodality: Current challenges for educational studies* (pp. 11–32). Rotterdam: Sense Publishers.
Blommaert, J., & Backus, A. (2013). Repertoires revisited: Knowing language in superdiversity. *Working Papers in Urban Language & Literacies*, 67.
Byrnes, H. (2006). Perspectives. Interrogating communicative competence as a framework for collegiate foreign language study. *The Modern Language Journal*, 90, 244–246.
Cope, B., & Kalantzis, M. (2009). "Multiliteracies": New literacies, new learning. *Pedagogies*, 4(3), 164–195.
Duranti, A. (1997). *Linguistic anthropology*. Cambridge: Cambridge University Press.
Early, M., Kendrick, M., & Potts, D. (2015). Multimodality: Out from the margins of English language teaching. *TESOL Quarterly*, 49(3), 447–460.
Goodwin, C. (2003). The body in action. In J. Coupland & R. Gwyn (Eds.), *Discourse, the body, and identity* (pp. 19–42). London: Palgrave-MacMillan.
Hall, J.K. (2011). *Teaching and researching language and culture*, 2nd ed. London: Pearson.
Hanks, W. F. (1996). *Language & communicative practices*. Colorado: Westview Press.
Jewitt, C. (2008). Multimodality and literacy in school classrooms. *Review of Research in Education*, 32(1), 241–267.
Jewitt, C. (2013). *Learning and communication in digital multimodal landscapes*. London: Institute of Education Press.
Jewitt, C., & Kress, G. (Eds.) (2003). *Multimodal literacy*. New York: Peter Lang.
Käänta, L. (2012). Teachers' embodied allocations in instructional interaction. *Classroom Discourse*, 3(2), 166–186.
Kress, G. (2010). *Multimodality: A social semiotic approach to contemporary communication*. London: Routledge.
Kress, G. (2014). The rhetorical work of shaping the semiotic world. In A. Archer & D. Newfield (Eds.), *Multimodal approaches to research and pedagogy: Recognition, resources, and access* (pp. 131–152). New York: Routledge.
Levinson, S. (2006). Cognition at the heart of human interaction. *Discourse Studies*, 8, 85–91.
Matthiessen, C. M. (2009). Meaning in the making: Meaning potential emerging from acts of meaning. *Language Learning*, 59(1), 206–229.
Mondada, L. (2016). Challenges of multimodality: Language and the body in social interaction. *Journal of Sociolinguistics*, 20(3), 336–366.
Mortensen, K. (2009). Establishing recipiency in pre-beginning position in the second language classroom. *Discourse Processes*, 46(5), 491–515.
New London Group. (1996). A pedagogy of multiliteracies: Designing social futures. *Harvard Educational Review*, 66, 60–92.
New London Group. (2000). A pedagogy of multiliteracies: Designing social futures. In B. Cope & M. M. Kalantzis (Eds.), *Multiliteracies: Literacy learning and design of social futures* (pp. 9–37). London: Routledge.

Ochs, E. (1996). Linguistic resources for socializing humanity. In J. Gumperz & S. Levinson (Eds.), *Rethinking linguistic relativity* (pp. 407–437). Cambridge: Cambridge University Press.

Rymes, B. (2010). Classroom discourse analysis: A focus on communicative repertoires. In N. Hornberger & S. McKay (Eds.), *Sociolinguistics and language education* (pp. 528–546). Tonawanda, NY: Multilingual Matters.

Rymes, B. (2012). Recontextualizing YouTube: From micro-macro to mass-mediated communicative repertoires. *Anthropology & Education Quarterly, 43*(2), 214–227.

Streeck, J., Goodwin, C., & LeBaron, C. (Eds.). (2011). *Embodied interaction: Language and body in the material world.* Cambridge University Press: New York.

Tomasello, M. (1999). *The cultural origins of human cognition.* Cambridge: Harvard University Press.

Chapter 4

L2 Learning Is Situated, and Attentionally and Socially Gated

Overview

As we discussed in Chapter 2, research on language from several fields has converged on findings about language knowledge. In contrast to a view of language as a fixed system of symbols and rules for their combination, current understandings reveal it to comprise complex, dynamic constructions. Learning these constructions is not simply the uptake of linguistic forms. Indeed, it is far more complex. It entails dynamic interactions between individual neurobiological and cognitive capabilities and three interdependent layers of social activity (Douglas Fir Group, 2016). At the micro level of social activity, individuals' emotional and general cognitive capabilities interact with social processes in ways that give shape to L2 learners' repertoires of semiotic resources. What is attended to at the micro level of social activity focuses learning. This level is represented by the white concentric circle, embedded within two larger circles, that is depicted in Chapter 1's Figure 1.1. In this chapter, we take a closer look at the micro level of learning.

Learning Is Situated

The learning of language is driven by the human need to communicate (Tomasello, 2008). Whether it is one's first, second, or third language that is being learned, language learning begins at the micro level of social activity. To state that language learning is situated and socially gated at this level means that it occurs as a matter of making meaning in shared activity with others within the social contexts of daily life (Lee, Mikesell, Joaquin, Mates, & Schumann, 2009; MacWhinney, 2012).

The scope of these contexts is wide-ranging and includes informal contexts such as gatherings with friends and family and more formal contexts such as educational classrooms, and professional and workplace settings. The activities that form part of these contexts can also range from very informal to formal. Informal activities include, for example, interacting face-to-face or via social media with friends and family and engaging in recreational pursuits. More formal activities include participating in classroom instructional interactions, engaging in professional meetings and other proceedings, taking part in civil and religious ceremonies and so on.

There are two key aspects of social experiences that contribute to the development of individual language knowledge at the micro level of social activity. One is the recurring nature of the experiences and the second is the distribution and frequency with which specific linguistic components of actions are encountered in the experiences. As individuals engage in their social experiences, they draw on a range of emotional and general cognitive capacities such as perception, association, and categorization. These capacities help to focus their attention on particular constructions and patterns of actions and to detect patterns in the use of the constructions, hypothesize about their form-meanings connections, test their understandings of the connections, categorize them and so on (Bybee, 2006; Goldberg, 1995, 2003). The more routine learners' social experiences are and the more frequent, predictable, and stable the uses of particular constructions are in the experiences, the more likely the constructions will become part of their repertoires.

Interactional Instinct

Emotion and motivation play significant roles in language learning at the micro level of social activity. Underpinning the emotional-motivational system is the *interactional instinct* (Lee et al., 2009; Schumann, 2010, 2013). This instinct is an innate attentional and motivational drive that pushes children to seek out and engage in emotionally rewarding, bonding relationships with their caregivers. These relationships make possible sufficient opportunities for children to be exposed to and participate in regular, routinized interactions with others. The intensely rewarding aspects of their bonds become part of their memories and serve as a template for subsequent affiliative relationships, and, along with the relationships, additional opportunities for interaction. For first language learners, these conditions ensure successful language learning (Lee et al., 2009; Schumann, 2013).

L2 learning relies on the same conditions of emotion, motivation, and opportunity. The interactional instinct can compel adolescent and adult L2 learners to seek out emotionally rewarding, motivating relationships with others who speak the language they are learning. The more positively they evaluate their potential interactions with others, the more effort L2 learners will make to participate in them and affiliate with others. However, while the interactional instinct guarantees that children in normal situations acquire their L1, L2 learning for adolescents

> **Quote 4.1 On Determining the Reward Potential of L2 Contexts of Action**
>
> To determine the reward potential that may be afforded by L2 contexts of action, humans evaluate them according to five dimensions: novelty, pleasantness, goal or need significance, coping potential, and self- and social image (Lee et al., 2009). This is part of regular brain functioning: Human brains "integrate 'emotional' (e.g., value, risk) and 'cognitive' computations (e.g., prediction error, attention allocation, action selection) in ways that support adaptive behavior" (Okon-Singer et al., 2015, p. 6). For L2 learners this may mean that the more they experience emotionally and motivationally positive evaluations of their anticipated and real interactions, the more effort they will make to participate in them and affiliate with others.
>
> Douglas Fir Group (2016, p. 28)

and adults is much more variable. This is because the older L2 learners are, not only are their social relationships more complicated, but also the intensity of motivation and emotional rewards they derive from such relationships in the L2 are likely to be diminished. For example, adult learners have extensive repertoires in their L1 that allow them to express and understand complex ideas, to build and sustain interpersonal relationships with others, and to participate in a wide range of social activities. The rewards they derive from these experiences are likely to be highly motivating. Without the semiotic resources in L2 that would allow them to participate in similar types of experiences, they are likely to be less motivated to seek out and sustain interactions within L2 contexts of interaction. Consequently, their opportunities for learning are also likely to be reduced. This is further explained by the Douglas Fir Group (2016) in Quote 4.1. There is a long history of research on motivation in L2 learning, driven by concerns with enhancing the conditions by which L2 learner motivation can be increased such that successful L2 learning can occur. The topic of motivation is discussed in more detail in Chapter 7.

Interaction Engine

Undergirded by the emotional-motivational platform of the interactional instinct is the *interaction engine* (Levinson, 2006; Schumann, Guvendir, & Joaquin, 2013). The term refers to the cognitive abilities and behavioral dispositions that predispose individuals to engage in collaborative social interactions (Enfield & Levinson, 2006; Levinson, 2006; Enfield & Sidnell, 2014). The interaction engine comprises several types of abilities and skills. Included are abilities to infer the motivations, stances, and intentions behind others' actions and what they understand about individuals' own actions. It also includes the abilities to recruit the attention of others and to share understandings of the situation at hand, skills for coordinating behaviors with others to achieve common goals, and the capacity for creating and interpreting communicative actions in multiple modes, i.e., gesture, gaze, and facial behaviors in addition to verbal modes simultaneously. This "core universal set of proclivities and abilities that human beings bring, by virtue of human nature, to the business of interaction" (Levinson, 2006, p. 40) is what makes interaction between individuals possible, and thus, provides the grounding for the emergence of language knowledge.

General Cognitive Abilities

Individual learners also bring to their experiences a set of general cognitive capabilities on which they draw to register their encounters with the various semiotic resources comprising their contexts of interaction. The set of capabilities includes abilities to select and attend to particular meaning-making components and their patterns of action, to perform statistically-based analyses on various kinds of patterns and sequences, and to create mappings or analogies and form schemas based on recurrent patterns (Tomasello, 2000, 2008). It is with these capabilities that individuals' attention is drawn to particular resources, and with which they detect patterns in their use, and hypothesize about and test understandings of their meanings in their experiences.

The Role of Input

The structure of the language environments in which language learners participate also plays a significant role in learning. Key factors include the distribution, frequency, and salience of sequences of actions and their specific linguistic constructions in the activities in which individuals are regularly engaged (Bybee, 2003; Boyd & Goldberg, 2009). Salience refers to the relative prominence of an item in the environment such that one's attention is attracted to it (Cintrón-Valentin & Ellis, 2016). The more frequent, consistent, and salient the use of particular form-meaning pairings is in the unfolding actions of the activities, and the more learners' attention is drawn to them, the more likely the constructions will be perceived and stored as cognitive representations of their experiences, and the more fluently individuals will access and use them. Likewise, the more frequent and salient the use of constructions is in particular contexts, the more individuals will associate the constructions with their contexts of use (Douglas Fir Group, 2016).

Two types of frequency have an effect on the development of an individual's L2 repertoire: *token frequency* and *type frequency* (Bybee, 1995, 2008; Bybee & Thompson, 2000; Bybee & Hopper, 2001; Ellis, 2006; Ellis & Collins, 2009; Tomasello, 2000). *Token frequency* has to do with how often a particular construction or set of constructions appears in the input; it leads to the preservation or entrenchment of single units. Single units can include words, phrases, and even entire clauses. The more frequently individuals are exposed to particular tokens, the more likely the items will become entrenched in their repertoires and accessed as whole units. Entrenchment refers to the strengthening of memory traces through repeated activation; high frequency constructions become highly entrenched (Roehr-Brackin, 2015). This is so regardless of how seemingly irregular the constructions are.

Boyland's (2001) study on the use of the English construction *X and I* is a good example of this. In her corpus of data, she found that the most frequently occurring pronoun with *I* is the pronoun *you* in the construction *X and I*, i.e., *you and I*. Because of the high frequency of the construction's use, she argues, speakers process the phrase as one unit. Thus, they are more apt to use the unit *you and I* after prepositions such as *between* and *from* rather than the grammatically prescribed object pronoun *me*, as in *between you and me* or *from you and me*. Idioms are another example of tokens. An idiom is a phrase or clause whose meaning cannot be deduced from any single component of the phrase or clause. They are often learned and stored as whole units. English phrases such as *twenty-four seven* and *a piece of cake*, and clauses such as *run around in circles* and *add insult to injury*, are examples of such idiomatic expressions. High frequency of use of such tokens in individuals' input promotes their entrenchment in individuals' repertoires.

Type frequency has to do with the frequency of patterns that call for different items in particular slots. These patterns, which are more abstract constructions, are considered productive patterns. This means that they can be used to generate a wide range of meaningful acts. The more frequently a pattern is used in an individual's linguistic environment, the more productive it is (Ellis, 2002). A pattern with high frequency in English is subject-verb-object (SVO), as in *I saw a movie* and *the child bought a toy*. What individuals extract from its frequent use and store in their repertoires is the SVO pattern, and they draw on the pattern to create new expressions. Another example of a highly frequent pattern in English is the regular past tense verb ending of *–ed* (*verb+ed*). This item is used to create past tense for thousands of different verbs, e.g., *guide, guided*; *help, helped*; *call, called*; and so on. The greater number of lexical items that occur in a certain position in a pattern, the more likely a general category of items will be created and the less likely the pattern will become associated with any particular lexical item (Bybee, 2010; Ellis & Larsen-Freeman, 2006).

Also key to learning are situational cues in the linguistic input that make salient and call individuals' attention to particular components and their form-meaning relationships. These include verbal cues such as repetitions, formulations, tone and pitch changes, and nonverbal cues such as gaze and gesture (Atkinson, 2014; Douglas Fir Group, 2016; Eskildsen & Wagner, 2015; Ibbotson, Lieven, & Tomasello, 2013). Emotion also plays an important role in cueing learners' attention to key aspects of their social contexts. Cues that are emotionally charged are more attention-getting than neutral cues, while negatively charged cues can hinder or block attention to them.

Individuals are active agents in this process. They use their interaction-engine and other cognitive capacities for sharing and directing joint attention to register and catalogue their experiences with language. As they engage in their recurring activities, they actively select and attend to specific kinds of information, locate patterns of form-meaning pairings, hypothesize about the motivations of others' actions, and test to see if their intended goals were met in their interactions. It is important to note that individuals' attention to these cues at the micro level of social activity is not uniform across learners as emotional, motivational, cognitive, and other factors can affect the salience of cues (Cintrón-Valentin & Ellis, 2016; Okon-Singer, Hendler, & Shackman, 2015). Depending on these factors and learners' prior experiences, what may be salient to some individuals in a particular social experience may not be to others. Resulting from the variable processes of learning are individually-based repertoires that are equally variable.

To recap, the more emotionally rewarding social activities are to individuals, the more routine, frequent, salient, and stable the occurrences of particular resources are in the activities, and the more individuals' attention is drawn to them, the more entrenched the resources become as cognitive–emotional representations of their experiences (Douglas Fir Group, 2016). It is learners' eventual internalization and self-regulated use of their resources for taking action in their social worlds that characterizes learning. All else being equal, the more extensive, complex, and emotionally rewarding the contexts of interaction become over time and the more enduring individuals' participation is in them, the more complex and enduring the resources comprising their repertoires will be.

Differences Between L1 and L2 Learning

The implications from findings on first language learning are fairly straightforward for L2 learning: the more exposure a learner has to frequently used, salient constructions, the greater the chance the constructions will be learned. However, while first and second language learners have access to the same mechanisms for learning at the micro level of social activity, L2 learning is, in fact, highly variable for several reasons (Cintrón-Valentin & Ellis, 2016; Ellis & Larsen-Freeman, 2006; MacWhinney, 2004; Schumann, 2013).

First, adolescent and adult learners come to L2 learning with firmly entrenched perceptual mechanisms and well-formed and entrenched constructions in their first language. The degree to which L2 constructions are similar to L1 constructions, the L1 can serve as the basis for learning the L2. However, despite any apparent similarities, differences in details between the L1 and L2 can block learners from perceiving these differences in the L2 (Ellis, 2006; Ellis & Sagarra, 2010; Five Graces Group, 2009). Blocking is a phenomenon of learned attention. That is to say, although there may be cues present in the L2 input for expressing meaning, they may be blocked from uptake by L2 learners because the cues learned in their L1s block their attention to the cues in the L2 (Ellis, 2015; Sagarra & Ellis, 2013).

It can also be the case that constructions in the L2 are of low salience, that is, difficult to detect, and thus difficult to learn. For example, for learners with English as their first language, preceding nouns with adjectives is an entrenched pattern of expression, e.g., *the blue house, the appreciated donation*. In other languages, such as Spanish, the adjectives conventionally follow nouns, e.g., *la casa azul, la donación apreciada*. Expressing such meanings using the conventions of the L2 can be difficult for the learners. Similarly, cues that are more salient in the L1 may overshadow or block cues in the L2. For example, lexical cues in the L1 that reliably reference time, such as *ayer* in Spanish, may block the acquisition of verb tense morphology when both cues for referencing time occur in the same utterance in the L2, such as the English expression *yesterday, I went to school* (Ellis, 2006; Ellis & Sagarra, 2010).

Another reason that L2 learning is more variable is because, as mentioned earlier, the social environment and conditions of learning are significantly different from those of a child acquiring a first language (Five Graces Group, 2009). Children learning their first language depend on an intense system of social support from their caregivers. In comparison, L2 learners have already been socialized into particular social activities and social groups and they may not have the same levels of support or motivations for engaging in L2 social groups and contexts of action. They may even desire to learn the L2 but lack the willingness to communicate with others using the language (MacIntyre, 2007). Even if they are motivated to engage with others who speak the L2, they may lack adequate exposure to a full range of L2 experiences, and thus have insufficient linguistic data from which to detect patterns (Bybee, 2008; Douglas Fir Group,

2016). It is useful to note that the relationship between learners' first and second languages is dynamic and reciprocal. This means that in the case where L2 learners' motivation for learning an L2 may be weak early on, learning experiences can increase their emotional and motivational attachments and result in reinforced connections to the second language, to their learning experiences and so on (Pavlenko, 2013).

Summary

Language learning begins at the micro level of social activity as we participate in recurrent activities with others within the social contexts of our daily lives. As we engage in our social experiences, we draw on a range of emotional and cognitive capacities that bring our attention to constructions in the making of meaning, allowing us to detect patterns in their use, hypothesize about their communicative meanings, test our understandings, and so on. Also playing a role are the cues used by more experienced participants to focus our attention on relevant meaning-making resources. The more routine our social experiences are and the more frequent, predictable, salient, and stable the uses of particular constructions are, the more likely the constructions will become part of our repertoires. Resulting from the ongoing process are individually-based organizations of language knowledge, i.e., collections of "largely prefabricated particulars" (Hopper, 1998, p. 164) that are "variable and probabilistic" (Bybee & Hopper, 2001, p. 219).

While L2 learners rely on the same processes they use to learn their first language, L2 learning for adolescents and adults is more variable. The more similar that L1 meaning-making constructions are to those in the L2, the easier it may be for L2 learners to learn them. However, even slight differences between L1 and L2 can complicate the learning of L2. Also more variable is L2 learners' motivation for seeking out opportunities to use the L2 with L2 speakers. However, while there are challenges to learning another language, they are not static or deterministic, but rather dynamic (Douglas Fir Group, 2016).

Implications for Understanding L2 Teaching

It is at the micro level of social activity where the detailed work of L2 learning occurs. From an understanding of L2 learning as situated, and attentionally and socially gated, we can derive four implications for understanding L2 teaching.

1 To *learn* another language one must be involved in contexts of interaction *using* the language. The inextricable link obtaining between L2 learning and use highlights the critical role that the contexts of L2 classrooms play in L2 learning. These contexts do not just simply

awaken what is already in learners, facilitating some kind of fixed, stable course of development. Rather, they give fundamental shape to the paths that learning takes and the compositions of learners' repertoires. To state another way, what learners take away from their classrooms in terms of their developing L2s is intimately tied to the kinds of contexts of use that teachers create in their interactions with learners. L2 teaching is inextricably, inexorably related to L2 learning.

2   No two L2 learners experience the same contexts of language use in exactly the same way. Learners in our classrooms come with different histories of L1 learning and use, and consequently different L1 repertoires. They also come with varying abilities to detect patterns (Douglas Fir Group, 2016), and varying levels of motivation for participating in L2 social contexts. Despite our best efforts to create rich L2 learning environments in our classrooms, L2 learners' trajectories of learning and their developing L2 repertoires will inevitably differ. This observation helps us understand *why* our L2 learners end up in different places at the end of a lesson, a unit, a semester, and at the end of the entire course.

3   The challenges of L2 learning for older L2 learners at the micro level of social activity notwithstanding, there is much we can do as teachers to assist them, particularly in recruiting their attention to components of the L2 that may be blocked or less salient. One way is to enhance the linguistic input to increase availability and accessibility of those components that may not be readily available (Collins, Trofimovich, White, Cardoso, & Horst, 2009). Integrating multiple modes of meaning making into the linguistic environment can also help to focus learners' attention. Finally, explicit instruction can increase their awareness of those components that they would otherwise ignore or miss. The matter of explicit instruction is taken up more fully in Chapter 8.

4   As L2 teachers, we are not solely responsible for designing a rich learning environment and supporting learners' development. L2 learners play an equally significant role. They need to be active in co-constructing L2 learning spaces in the classroom and in designing projects that push them to maximize their learning opportunities (Eskildsen & Theodórsdóttir, 2017). For them to do this work, learners need to be positioned as agentive project makers and problem-solvers. The matter of individual agency is discussed in more detail in Chapter 7.

Pedagogical Activities

In this series of pedagogical activities, you will engage in different *knowledge processes* that will assist you in relating to and making sense of the concepts that inform our understanding of *L2 learning as situated, and attentionally and socially gated*.

Experiencing

A. Salience and Learning

Recall your most salient memories of learning a second language. Describe the contexts, the materials, the people involved, the places and so on. What did you find yourself paying attention to? What difficulties did you experience? Compare your memories to those of a classmate and together construct a Venn diagram that represents the relationships between your memories. Figure 4.1 contains examples of Venn diagrams. What can you conclude about the links between salience and L2 learning?

B. Classroom Contexts of Learning

Summarize four or five main ideas from your reading of the chapter. Based on your summary, design a tool that can be used to gather data on how language teaching is accomplished in a language classroom. The purpose is not to evaluate the teaching, but to observe various features of the learning environment that the teacher creates through the spatial arrangement of desks and chairs, her/his interactions with learners and her/his use of written or visual materials, digital technologies, and other artifacts. If you cannot find a classroom near you, search the internet for a

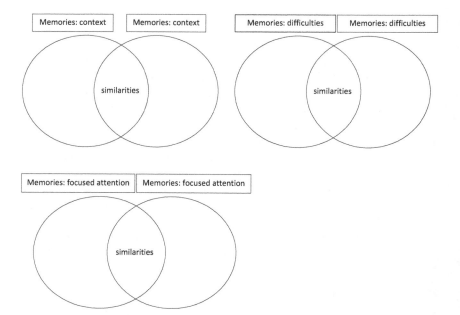

Figure 4.1 Examples of Venn diagrams.

video of a language classroom. To get enough data, the video should be at least six minutes long. Summarize your findings and compare them with those of others. What can you conclude about the relationship between teaching and the design of language classroom learning environments?

Conceptualizing

A. Concept Development

Select two of the concepts listed in Box 4.1. Craft a definition of each of the two concepts in your own words. Create one or two concrete examples of each concept that you have either experienced first-hand or can imagine. Pose one or two questions that you still have about the concepts and develop a way to gather more information.

Box 4.1 Concepts: L2 learning is situated, and attentionally and socially gated

(blocked) attention
domain general cognitive capabilities
interaction engine
interactional instinct

token frequency
type frequency
salience

B. Concept Development

Choose one of the concepts you selected from the list in Box 4.1 on which to gather additional information. Using the internet search for information about the concept. Create a list of five or so facts about it. These can include names of scholars who study the concept, studies that have been done on the concept along with their findings, visual images depicting the concept, and so on. Create a concept web that visually records the information you gathered from your explorations.

Analyzing

A. Contexts of L2 Learning

The article by Eskildsen and Theodórsdóttir (2017) reports on two cases of L2 learning, one inside the classroom and one outside, in the "wild", showing how different learning environments were constructed in the two contexts. Read the article and then write a report that 1. identifies the main argument, 2. describes the features of each learning context, 3. summarizes the findings from each case, and 4. concludes with a discussion of what you consider to be two or three significant implications for your own teaching.

B. Classroom Materials

Language textbooks play a central role in classroom L2 learning. Given their importance, it would be useful to conduct an analysis of their content in terms of how well they appear to support usage-based understandings of language and learning. In pairs or small groups, select two or three textbooks that are used in a language course you are familiar with or aspire to teach. It can be for any grade and any group of L2 learners. Create a list of criteria about language and L2 learning derived from the material in Chapters 2, 3, and 4 to use in the analysis of the textbooks. Once your criteria are determined, use the list to evaluate the content of each textbook. Compile your results and prepare a multimodal presentation on them for the class.

Applying

A. Classroom Contexts of Learning

Building on your report of the article by Eskildsen and Theodórsdóttir (2017), together with your classmates, in pairs or small groups, brainstorm at least four ways that you can build links between learning spaces inside and outside of the classroom. Design a multimodal project that represents these ways and, together with the rest of the class, consider ways to disseminate your projects to a wider audience. Suggestions include holding in-class presentations and seeking feedback from your classmates via online blogs, holding a workshop for other language teachers at your university, presenting your projects at a local or statewide professional organization and uploading your projects to a language teacher website that allows teachers to share their work. One such site is Share My Lesson, where members can contribute content and share ideas (https://sharemylesson.com).

B. Learning Outside of the Classroom

This activity is an extension of the previous exercise. Design a project for your learners that takes them into the community for extended opportunities to use the target language. Use the case of Anna, presented in the article by Eskildsen and Theodórsdóttir (2017), as an example. If the language you are teaching or hope to teach is not prevalent in the community, design a project that utilizes online social media. For a list of social media sites, visit this site: https://en.wikipedia.org/wiki/List_of_social_networking_websites.

Once the project is completed, consider ways to share your project with others.

References

Atkinson, D. (2014). Language learning in mindbodyworld: A sociocognitive approach to second language acquisition. *Language Teaching*, 47(4), 467–483.

Boyd, J., & Goldberg, A. E. (2009). Input effects within a constructionist framework. *The Modern Language Journal*, 93, 418–429.

Boyland, J. T. (2001). Cognitive processes that account for pronoun usage. *Frequency and the Emergence of Linguistic Structure*, 45, 383.

Bybee, J. (1995). Regular morphology and the lexicon. *Language and Cognitive Processes*, 10, 425–455.

Bybee, J. (2003). Mechanisms of change in grammaticalization: The role of frequency. In R. D. Janda & B. D. Joseph (Eds.), *Handbook of historical linguistics* (pp. 602–623). Oxford: Blackwell.

Bybee, J. (2006). From usage to grammar: The mind's response to repetition. *Language*, 82(4), 711–733.

Bybee, J. (2008). Usage-based grammar and second language acquisition. In P. Robinson & N. Ellis (Eds.), *Handbook of cognitive linguistics and second language acquisition* (pp. 216–236). London: Routledge.

Bybee, J. (2010). *Language, usage and cognition*. Cambridge: Cambridge University Press.

Bybee, J., & Hopper, P. (2001). Introduction to frequency and the emergence of linguistic structure. In J. Bybee and P. Hopper (Eds.), *Frequency and the emergence of linguistic structure* (pp. 1–24). Amsterdam: John Benjamins.

Bybee, J., & Thompson, S. (2000). Three frequency effects in syntax. *Berkeley Linguistic Society*, 23, 65–85.

Cintrón-Valentín, M. C., & Ellis, N. C. (2016). Salience in second language acquisition: Physical form, learner attention, and instructional focus. *Frontiers in Psychology*, 7, article 1284.

Collins, L., Trofimovich, P., White, J., Cardoso, W., & Horst, M. (2009). Some input on the easy/difficult grammar question: An empirical study. *The Modern Language Journal*, 93(3), 336–353.

Douglas Fir Group (2016). A transdisciplinary framework for SLA in a multilingual world. *The Modern Language Journal*, 100, 19–47.

Ellis, N. C. (2002). Frequency effects in language processing: A review with implications for theories of implicit and explicit language acquisition. *Studies in Second Language Acquisition*, 24(2), 143–188.

Ellis, N. C. (2006). Language acquisition as rational contingency learning. *Applied Linguistics*, 27(1), 1–24.

Ellis, N. C. (2015). Implicit and explicit learning: Their dynamic interface and complexity. In P. Rebuschat (Ed.), *Implicit and explicit learning of languages* (pp. 3–23). Amsterdam: John Benjamins.

Ellis, N. C., & Collins, L. (2009). Input and second language acquisition: The roles of frequency, form, and function. *The Modern Language Journal, 93*(3), 329–336.

Ellis, N. C., & Larsen-Freeman, D. (2006). Language emergence: Implications for applied linguistics. Introduction to the special issue. *Applied Linguistics, 27*(4), 558–589.

Ellis, N. C., & Sagarra, N. (2010). The bounds of adult language acquisition: Blocking and learned attention. *Studies in Second Language Acquisition, 32*(4), 553–580.

Enfield, N. & Levinson, S. (Eds.) (2006). *Roots of human sociality: Culture, cognition, and interaction*. London: Berg.

Enfield, N., & Sidnell, J. (2014). Language presupposes an enchronic infrastructure for social interaction. *The social origins of language*, 92–104.

Eskildsen, S. W., & Theodórsdóttir, G. (2017). Constructing L2 learning spaces: Ways to achieve learning inside and outside the classroom. *Applied Linguistics, 38*(2), 143–164.

Eskildsen, S. W., & Wagner, J. (2015). Embodied L2 construction learning. *Language Learning, 65*(2), 268–297.

Five Graces Group. (2009). Language is a complex adaptive system: Position paper. *Language Learning, 59*(s1), 1–26.

Goldberg, A. E. (1995). *Constructions: A construction grammar approach to argument structure*. Chicago: University of Chicago Press.

Goldberg, A. E. (2003). Constructions: A new theoretical approach to language. *Trends in Cognitive Sciences, 7*(5), 219–224.

Hopper, P. (1998). Emergent grammar. In M. Tomasello (Ed.), *New psychology of language* (pp. 155–175). Mahwah, NJ: Erlbaum.

Ibbotson, P., Lieven, E. V. M., & Tomasello, M. (2013). The attention-grammar interface: Eye-gaze cues structural choice in children and adults. *Cognitive Linguistics, 24*(3), 457–481.

Lee, N., Mikesell, L., Joaquin, A. D. L., Mates, A. W., & Schumann, J. H. (2009). *The interactional instinct: The evolution and acquisition of language*. Oxford: Oxford University Press.

Levinson, S. (2006). On the human "interaction engine". In N. Enfield & S. Levinson (Eds.), *Roots of human sociality* (pp. 39–69). London: Berg.

MacIntyre, P. D. (2007). Willingness to communicate in the second language: Understanding the decision to speak as a volitional process. *The Modern Language Journal, 91*(4), 564–576.

MacWhinney, B. (2004). A multiple process solution to the logical problem of language acquisition. *Journal of Child Language, 31*, 883–914.

MacWhinney, B. (2012). The logic of the unified model. In S. Gass & A. Mackey (Eds.), *The Routledge handbook of second language acquisition* (pp. 211–227). London: Routledge.

Okon-Singer, H., Hendler, T., Pessoa, L., & Shackman, A. J. (2015). The neurobiology of emotion–cognition interactions: Fundamental questions and strategies for future research. *Frontiers in Human Neuroscience, 9*, article 58.

Pavlenko, A. (2013). The affective turn in SLA: From "affective factors" to "language desire" and "commodification of affect". In D. Gabryś-Barker and J. Bielska (Eds.), *Affective dimension in second language acquisition* (pp. 211–225). Bristol: Multilingual Matters.

Roehr-Brackin, K. (2015). Long-term development in an instructed adult L2 learner: Usage-based and complexity theory applied. In T. Cadierno & S.W. Eskildsen (Eds.), *Usage-based perspectives on second language learning* (pp. 181–206). Berlin: de Gruyter.

Sagarra, N., & Ellis, N. C. (2013). From seeing adverbs to seeing verbal morphology: Language Experience and adult acquisition of L2 tense. *Studies in Second Language Acquisition, 35*(2), 261–290.

Schumann, J. H. (2010). Applied linguistics and the neurobiology of language. In R. Kaplan (Ed.), *The Oxford handbook of applied linguistics* (pp. 244–260). Oxford: Oxford University Press.

Schumann, J. H. (2013). Societal responses to adult difficulties in L2 acquisition: Toward an evolutionary perspective on language acquisition. *Language Learning, 63*(1), 190–209.

Schumann, J. H., Güvendir, E., & Joaquin, A. D. L. (2013). The interactional instinct and related perspectives. In A. Joaquin & J. Schumann (Eds.), *Exploring the interactional instinct* (pp. 256–268). Oxford: Oxford University Press.

Tomasello, M. (2000). The item-based nature of children's early syntactic development. *Trends in Cognitive Sciences, 4*, 156–163.

Tomasello, M. (2008). *Origins of human cognition*. Cambridge, MA: MIT Press.

Chapter 5

L2 Learning Is Mediated and Embodied

Overview

Recall, in Chapter 4, it was stated that facilitating learners' emotional-cognitive processes in noticing, ordering, representing, and remembering semiotic resources specific to their contexts of interaction are resources used by others, typically more experienced participants, to call attention to the relevant resources and assist learners in noticing and remembering them (Ellis & Larsen-Freeman, 2006; Tomasello, 2003, 2008). A term used to refer to the actions by which such work is accomplished is mediation. The specific resources that are used to mediate learners' involvement in their contexts of interaction are tied, at the meso level of social activity, to particular sociocultural groups, such as families, friends, neighborhoods, and particular social institutions such as schools, places of work, recreational clubs, and so on. The process by which learning is mediated in these varied contexts is referred to as language socialization. In this chapter, we examine the concept of language socialization and what research has shown about L2 socialization, and we take a closer look at understandings of L2 learning as mediated and embodied.

Language Socialization

A great deal of empirical support on the links between the sociocultural institutions within which contexts of interaction are situated and the development of learners' repertoires comes from the field of study known as *language socialization*. The genesis of this field is credited to two renowned linguistic anthropologists, Elinor Ochs and Bambi Schieffelin (Ochs, 1988; Ochs & Schieffelin, 1984, 2008; Schieffelin & Ochs, 1986), who undertook research on language development among children in several different cultural communities. This research has its roots in the work of Dell Hymes (1962, 1964), also a distinguished linguistic anthropologist, who, in the 1960s, proposed a theory of language that posited social function to be the source from which linguistic units are formed (see Chapter 2). Hymes called his theory of language a socially constituted linguistics and explained that the term "socially constituted" expresses the view that "social function gives form to the ways in which linguistic features are encountered in actual life" (Hymes, 1974, p. 196).

Hymes' theory foreshadows current usage-based understandings of the inextricable relationship between linguistic form and social function. And, while Hymes' own research did not specifically address the issue of language development, it informed large programs of research on the cross-cultural study of the development of children's language that began in the late 1960s and continued steadily through the 1970s and well into the 1980s (e.g., Ervin-Tripp & Mitchell-Kernan, 1977; Heath, 1983; Slobin, 1967, 1985). This program included studies by Ochs and Schieffelin on the language development of children in Western Samoan and Kaluli communities (Ochs, 1988; Ochs & Schieffelin, 1984, 2008; Schieffelin & Ochs, 1986). Their studies revealed empirical links between community beliefs about language use, the language activities in which caregivers and children regularly engaged, and the specific kinds of linguistic resources children eventually acquired. Ochs and Schieffelin concluded that in their activities with caregivers, children were not only being socialized into particular ways of using and interpreting linguistic resources for making meaning. At the same time, they were being socialized into local understandings on the appropriateness of the resources and their value for self- and other-expression. The findings from this program of research formed the basis of the language socialization approach.

A key premise of this approach is that the process of language development is embedded in and constitutive of the process of becoming socialized into competent participation in the social activities of one's social groups by more knowledgeable members (Ochs & Schieffelin, 2017). More knowledgeable members can include parents, siblings and other family members, other caregivers outside of the family, and peers. The social activities that novices are socialized into are culturally-mediated, conventionalized activities that are important to the accomplishment of the daily lives of their social groups. For young children, daily activities typically include those occurring at home, for example, during meal times and play times, and during bedtime routines that may include recounting the day's events, reading books, and saying prayers. For older children and adults, activities include those typically found in schools, places of worship, community center programs, and so on (Baquedano-Lopez & Kattan, 2008).

Novices are socialized into their activities and the semiotic resources used to accomplish the activities through more experienced members' regular, extended use of the resources and their guided assistance in helping novices to use the resources on their own. In other words, they are socialized *through* language to *use* language. It is not only what is encoded in language forms, but more importantly, how meaning is constructed in social action that shapes development (Hall, 2011). With time and experience in their activities, novices become adept at using the semiotic resources for making meaning on their own.

In the processes of socialization, the development of language is intertwined with the development of social and cultural knowledge. Ochs (1996, p. 409) explains:

> the two processes are intertwined from the moment a human being enters society (at birth, in the womb, or at whatever point local philosophy defines as 'entering society'). Each process facilitates the other as children and other novices come to a perspective on social life in part through signs and come to understand signs in part through social experience.

Through experts' regular, extended use of language and other semiotic resources novices become adept at using and knowing the semiotic resources and their cultural meanings specific to the social activities of their social groups. As discussed in Chapter 4, factors that are key to focusing novices' attention on relevant resources are cues used by more expert participants that call the novices' attention to them. Such assistance can take many forms and includes the use of verbal and nonverbal actions that explicitly direct learners' attention to the semiotic resources and their meaning-making potentials, and other less explicit actions including repetitions, recyclings, and recasts of one another's words; tone, intonation, and pitch changes; eye gaze and gesture; and so on. These forms of assistance are considered *mediational means* and the process by which they are used in interaction is *mediation*. We discuss these terms in more detail below.

As children and other novices are socialized into the semiotic resources of their social activities, they also develop understandings of the range of social actions by which the activities are accomplished and of the kinds of social identities and roles, and relationships with others that the activities make possible. They also develop understandings of the expected abilities and responsibilities that are considered characteristic of their identities and role relationships, and the options available to them for using the resources to take action. More generally, they develop understandings about the sociocultural importance of the activities to their social groups. In the process of being socialized, learners are not passive recipients. As individual agents, they play an active role in that they have the capacity to embrace, resist, and transform the social worlds into which they are socialized (Ochs, 1996; Ochs & Schieffelin, 2008, 2017). The topic of individual agency is discussed in more detail in Chapter 7.

While much of the early research was concerned with the socialization of children and adolescents, as Ochs and Schieffelin (2008) make clear, the process is not limited to early childhood but rather is a lifespan experience. It "characterizes our human interactions throughout adulthood as we become socialized into novel activities, identities and objects relevant to work, family, recreation civic, religious, and other environments in increasingly globalized communities" (ibid.: 11).

Indexicality

A core concept of the language socialization approach is *indexicality*. Indexicality refers to the phenomenon whereby real-world uses of semiotic resources index or invoke particular meanings depending on their contexts of use (Hanks, 1999; Ochs, 1996). As discussed in Chapter 3, meanings of resources are not created anew every time they are used. Rather, they come to us with meanings already embedded within them, with meanings that have developed from their past uses by particular individuals in particular contexts for particular purposes, which, in turn, are shaped by diverse cultural, historical, and institutional forces.

Dimensions of meaning embedded in our semiotic resources include the social acts and contexts of use the resources typically invoke and the social identities of the participants involved in uses of the resources. Identities encompass all dimensions of social personhood including social groups, roles, and relationships. Also embedded in our resources are particular affective and epistemic stances toward the acts, contexts, and identities invoked by their uses, and larger institutional values about their uses. *Affective stance* refers to feelings, dispositions, and degrees of emotional intensity. *Epistemic stance* concerns degrees of certainty of one's knowledge and beliefs. Uses of our semiotic resources at any moment *index* or point to those meanings and the contexts of past use that are conventionally associated them (Ochs & Schieffelin, 2017).

Take the example of the English clause *"how are you"*. For many social groups, it is a typical greeting, offered in more formal social or professional settings such as workplace celebrations, conferences, meetings, and job interviews, where a greeting is expected to occur, such as when two people first come into contact with each other. It also signals possible identities of the participants as adults, or, at least, not as children, who may or may not know each other and a formal stance, i.e., attitude, taken by the participants toward each other and their context of action. The meanings change when the constructions *"hey, man"* or *"yo"* are used. These constructions can also be typical greetings, but they index different types of contexts, more informal settings, and different identities of and relationships between the participants, likely young adults.

As another example of indexicality, consider the English expression *"raise your hands"*. For many, it invokes the context of a classroom and the unequal role relationship that typically obtains between teachers and students, in which teachers have the authority to issue such a directive to students to manage how they bid for turns in their instructional activity. It is rarely used outside that context except, perhaps, to index a stance of humor, irony, or even repression toward someone or a situation. For example, its use in a meeting of peers serves to evoke the classroom context and a teacher-student relationship between the person issuing the directive and the rest of the members of the meeting. It may be that the person issuing the directive means to create a hierarchical relationship with his peers and thereby to index a repressive stance toward them. Alternatively, the person may be using it to index a humorous stance toward the fact that no one at the meeting is talking or that several people are overlapping their turns in a bid for the floor. In either case, its use indexes its contexts of past use and social identities and role relationships of those who are conventionally associated with it.

The process of invoking meaning is what Ochs refers to as *linguistic indexing*, and the cues used in the process are called *linguistic indexes* or *indexicals*. These cues "either alone or in sets, either directly or indirectly, and either retrospectively, prospectively or currently, establish contexts and as such are powerful socializing structures" (Ochs, 1988 p. 227). Understanding the semiotic resources of one's contexts of action necessarily involves understanding their conventional social meanings, that is, their *indexical potentials*. Likewise, understanding social order involves knowing how such order is instantiated, that is, knowing which resources to use to point to and make relevant particular aspects of one's sociocultural worlds such as relevant social identities and role relationships. Central to the process of individual socialization, then, is learning to connect the semiotic resources used in one's social activities to their indexical meanings.

Socialization is not, however, a uni-directional process, from experienced members to novices. Novices are active contributors. While our resources are "socio-historical product[s]" (Ochs, 1996, p. 416), they are also tools for transforming social order. As Ochs explains in Quote 5.1, a key focus of research on language socialization has been on the identification of semiotic resources and the sociocultural meanings that are indexed in their uses by which novices are socialized into their social groups and, more generally, their social worlds.

L2 Socialization

L2 socialization is based on the same principles as L1 socialization. What adds complexity is the fact that adolescents and adults who are

Quote 5.1 Semiotic Resources as Tools of Reproduction and Transformation

While language is a socio-historical product, language is also an instrument for forming and transforming social order. Interlocutors actively use language as a semiotic tool (Vygotsky, 1978) to either reproduce social forms and meanings or produce novel ones. In reproducing historically accomplished structures, interlocutors may use conventional forms in conventional ways to constitute the local social situation. For example, they may use a conventional form in a conventional way to call into play a particular gender identity. In other cases, interlocutors may bring novel forms to this end or use existing forms in innovative ways. In both cases, interlocutors wield language to (re)constitute their interlocutory environment. Every social interaction in this sense has the potential for both cultural persistence and change, and past and future are manifest in the interactional present.

Ochs (1996, p. 416)

being socialized into their L2 social worlds come already possessing diverse repertoires of semiotic resources, cultural traditions, and community affiliations (Duff, 2007, 2011). In addition, they bring different motivations and aspirations for learning another language. For example, some may move to another region or country to seek better jobs or educational opportunities, bringing with them social, financial, and other resources they acquired from past experiences. Others may come with limited resources, having fled conflict in their own countries. Their different motives may lead to differential access to opportunities for socialization into the social activities of their new communities, with some facing limited or even nonexistent opportunities while others are welcomed and given full access to L2 learning opportunities and support in the processes of socialization.

The processes of socialization in formal learning contexts such as those in schools and in adult and community programs further complicate the processes of socialization by the fact that groups of learners in these places are typically heterogeneous in age, education background, linguistic background, work experiences, and country of origin. Socialization under such conditions often leads not to the reproduction of L2 cultural and communicative practices but, instead, can take many paths. It can lead to the creation of hybrid practices, identities, and values, to incomplete or partial appropriation of the

L2, or to rejection of target norms and practices (Duff, 2007, 2008; Duff & May, 2017). Much L2 socialization research has addressed these issues in relation to L2 schooling contexts. This topic is taken up in Chapter 8.

Learning How to Mean

Complementing the language socialization approach to the study of language development is the work of Michael Halliday (1973, 1993). A world-renowned linguist, Halliday developed a language-based theory of learning that was based in large part on data he gathered from his own child during the period covering the child's growth from nine to 18 months. A key premise of his theory is that learning is a semiotic process of learning how to make meaning, with language being "the prototypical form of human semiotic" (1993, p. 93).

Like the language socialization approach, Halliday's theory considers language and culture learning to be mutually constitutive. Language is considered to be the quintessential semiotic resource that enables its users to learn the knowledge, practices, beliefs, and values of their culture. Halliday (1978, p. 9) explains:

> Language is the main channel through which the patterns of living are transmitted to him, through which he learns to act as a member of a 'society' – in and through the various social groups, the family, the neighbourhood, and so on – and to adopt its 'culture', its modes of thought and action, its beliefs and its values.

Based on his theory of language, Halliday developed an approach to the study of language use called *systemic functional linguistics*. The framework is *systemic* in that it considers language to be a network of interrelated systems of semiotic potentials. It is *functional* in that it seeks to account for the semiotic meanings of the forms used in particular contexts and to link these meanings to larger social structures. The purpose of such a framework is to understand the different purposes for which language forms are used within and across textual contexts, and "why a text means what it does, and why it is valued at it is" (Halliday, 1994: xxix). Halliday's work has informed a great deal of educational research that is based on the premise that language learning in schools is about "learning how to mean in new and different ways" (Byrnes, 2008, p. 6).

James Martin and his colleagues (e.g., Christie, 2008; Christie & Martin, 2007; Martin, 2006, 2009) have applied the framework of systemic functional linguistics to the development of the concept of *genre*, defining it as "a socially sanctioned means of constructing and negotiating meanings" (Christie, 2008, p. 29). The framework, together with the concept of genre, have been applied to the development of a genre-based pedagogy for reading and writing whose aim is to develop in learners a level of literacy that includes learner awareness of the meaning-making consequences of different linguistic resources as they are used in different subject matters. Matthiessen (2009), in Quote 5.2, explains the significance of language learning to learning how to mean.

> **Quote 5.2 Learning How to Mean**
>
> When people learn languages, they build up their own personalized meaning potentials as part of the collective meaning potential that constitutes the language, and they build up these personal potentials by gradually expanding their own registerial repertoires—their own shares in the collective meaning potential. As they expand their own registerial repertoires, they can take on roles in a growing range of contexts, becoming semiotically more empowered and versatile.
>
> Matthiessen (2009, p. 223)

Learning Is Mediated and Embodied

The theory of human development advanced by Lev S. Vygotsky, a Soviet psychologist, also considers socialization to be key to language development. A central premise of Vygotsky's (1981) theory, often referred to as sociocultural theory, locates the source of higher forms of mental functioning in social relationships. Development does not proceed from individual mind to social relationships but "toward *individualization* of social functions (transformation of social functions into psychological functions)" (Vygotsky, 1989: 61). He goes on to state:

> Any function in the child's cultural development appears twice, or on two planes. First it appears on the social plane, and then on the psychological plane. First it appears between people as an interpsychological category, and then within the child as an intrapsychological category... Social relations or relations among people genetically underlie all higher functions and their relationships.
>
> (Vygotsky, 1981, p. 163)

Vygotsky's work has had a significant impact on studies of L2 learning in classrooms. This work is discussed in more depth in Chapter 8. Here we take a closer look at the notions of mediation and mediational means. Understanding the role of mediation and the relationships between social activity, semiotic resources and other mediational means, and the development of higher mental functions are main concerns of Vygotsky's theory of development (1978, 1987).

A key premise of Vygotsky's theory is that learning takes place in the processes of socialization as children learn to use semiotic resources and other cultural resources to construct, represent, and remember their social worlds in their interactions with others. The semiotic resources serve to regulate, i.e., mediate novices' developing understandings of their worlds, their relationships with others, and their own mental processes (Lantolf, 2000). Also mediating individuals' development is the assistance provided by more knowledgeable others to the novices in transforming the social resources into individual tools for use.

Mediational Means

In this capacity, the semiotic resources that are used for making meaning are considered *mediational means* or "the 'carriers' of sociocultural patterns and knowledge" (Wertsch, 1994, p. 204). In addition to linguistic constructions, mediational means can include computational resources such as computers and calculators, graphic resources such as diagrams, maps and drawings, artifacts and tools such as books, clocks, hammers, writing systems, and writing devices. Even physical objects and their spatial arrangements, such as those of classrooms, and environmental structures such as road signs, traffic lights, and street grids mediate individuals' participation in their social worlds.

Mediational means then are the design tools of our social activities and we use them to instantiate, represent, and remember our involvement in them. We use calendars, for example, to help us remember when events will take place and to organize our commitments; we use maps to help us get from one place to another; and we use diagrams and drawings to help us visualize spatial and other kinds of arrangements. In theory, mediational means can be anything that is used to make meaning in social activities of social groups.

In the ways that the mediational means are used in individuals' social worlds, they give shape not only to the settings within which development occurs, but, more importantly, to the paths that individual development takes. In other words, the means themselves and the ways in which they are used in the processes of socialization do not simply awaken what is already in the mind of individuals, enhancing an otherwise fixed course of development. Rather, they fundamentally shape and transform it. The resulting repertoires of resources reflect at the same time individuals' "socialization and individuation" (Williams, 1977, p. 37). Indeed, as Vygotsky argues, it is through the processes of socialization that we "grow into the intellectual world of those around us" (1978, p. 88). Vygotsky explains this in more detail in Quote 5.3.

Quote 5.3 The Role of Mediational Means in Development

The greatest characteristic feature of child development is that this development is achieved under particular conditions of interactions with the environment, where the ideal and final form (ideal in the sense that it acts as a model for that which should be achieved at the end of the developmental period; and final in the sense that it represents what the child is supposed to attain at the end of its development) is not only already present and from the very start in contact with the child, but actually interacts and exerts a real influence on the primary form, on the first steps of the child's development. Something which is only supposed to take shape at the very end of development, somehow influences the very first steps in this development.

Vygotksy (1994, p. 344)

Alongside this body of research has been growing interest in documenting the *embodied resources* by which learning in mediated in L2 learning contexts. Embodied resources are nonverbal bodily means for taking action such as gestures, facial expressions, gaze, head movements, body movements and postures, and so on. In Chapter 8 we examine more closely the mediational role of instructional practices found in classrooms. Here we summarize findings on the specific role of an embodied resource, gesture, in mediating learning.

One research direction has focused on how teachers use gestures to mediate student learning of particular linguistic constructions (e.g., Belhiah, 2013; Churchill, Okada, Nishino, & Atkinson, 2010; Eskildsen & Wagner, 2013, 2015; Hudson, 2011; Matsumoto & Dobs, 2017; Smotrova & Lantolf, 2013; van Compernolle & Smotrova, 2014). For example, Matsumoto and Dobs (2017) show how a teacher's use of gestures in a university-level ESL class helped to make abstract grammatical concepts concrete and visible to students. They further showed that the gestures were appropriated by the students as resources to demonstrate their developing understandings of the concepts.

Another strand of research on gesture has examined its use by students to mediate theirs and others' participation in group tasks (e.g., Olsher, 2004; Mori & Hayashi, 2006; van Compernolle & Williams, 2011). For example, Olsher (2004) examined how gestures and other embodied behaviors served as interactional resources for a group of students in an EFL classroom working on a small group activity. He found that, in addition to pointing gestures, which were used to direct attention to an object or person as the project work unfolded, gestures were combined with other embodied resources to demonstrate learners' understandings and thereby complete turns in the accomplishment of their project. Together, studies on embodied resources such as gestures in L2 contexts of learning establish their intrinsic roles in the doing of teaching, i.e., in mediating learners' development, and, in their use by students, in mediating and demonstrating their own learning.

Summary

The social worlds into which children are born are "saturated with social and cultural forces, predilections, symbols, ideologies, and practices" (Ochs & Schieffelin, 2017, p. 6). Predicated on this premise, a great deal of research on L1 language socialization has revealed how children's language learning is intimately tied to the processes of being socialized into their social worlds. In the process, they learn how to mean, that is, to connect the semiotic resources used in their social activities to their indexical meanings, and how to use the resources to recreate their contexts of use, including the beliefs and values ascribed to the resources. L2 learning is based on the same principles as L1 socialization. However, the processes and outcomes are much more complicated for adolescents and adults as they come to their L2 contexts of learning having been socialized into wide-ranging multilingual, multimodal activities as part of their upbringing in their first language(s) social groups and institutions.

The concepts of indexicality, mediation, and mediational means are useful tools for understanding the links between the meanings of semiotic resources and their contexts of use, how their uses recreate their meanings and how, as mediational means, the resources mediate the processes and outcomes of socialization. Research on the role played by embodied resources such as gestures in mediating L2 learning reveals that they are as central to the processes of learning as verbal means are.

Implications for Understanding L2 Teaching

At the meso level of social activity, L2 learning happens through the processes of socialization, whereby learners' participation is mediated by wide-ranging multimodal, multilingual, and embodied semiotic resources. From an understanding of learning as mediated and embodied, we can derive three implications for understanding L2 teaching.

1. L2 classrooms are significant socializing contexts, L2 teachers are significant agents of socialization, and the resources we use to teach are significant mediational means. The means include written and digital materials such as textbooks, images, and videos, objects, the various types of instructional activities, and even the spatial arrangements of our classrooms, in addition to language. The decisions we make, then, in terms of what to teach, how to teach it, what counts as student participation and displays of learning are consequential to the learning paths our learners take and to their outcomes in terms of their developing L2 repertoires. Indeed, L2 teaching is highly demanding, sophisticated, and consequential professional work.
2. L2 teaching, i.e., mediating L2 learning, is accomplished by "exploiting a large array of multimodal resources, mobilized and packaged in an emergent, incremental, dynamic way" (Mondada, 2014, p. 140). Significant components of this array are our embodied resources, which, in addition to gestures, include facial expressions, body positionings and movements, and eye gaze. These resources are integrated holistically with speech, with their meanings defined locally, within the contexts of the unfolding activity. Gestures in particular play a significant role in mediating teaching and learning. Gestures display additional information to learners, which they can use to make sense of teachers' actions. Their use by learners provide additional information to us, as teachers, about their developing understandings. Understanding their integral role in the processes of L2 socialization is significant to understanding the complexities of L2 teaching.
3. The processes of socialization are equally important to the professional development of teachers. Our development as teachers reaches back to the thousands of hours we have spent as students in classrooms, observing and evaluating their teachers. Lortie (1975) labeled this "apprenticeship by observation". It also takes place informally, in interactions we have had with stakeholders such as parents and students, and outside of the profession, with family and friends. It has also occurred through exposure to portrayals of teachers in media such as movies and television shows. By the time we begin our formal preparation, we have already internalized understandings and beliefs about classroom teaching and learning, and about teachers and students. These understandings are highly influential to the trajectories that our professional socialization takes in our teacher preparation programs, and in interactions

with our professors, mentor teachers, and peer teachers. Developing expertise in teaching demands continual critical reflection on our beliefs and on how they inform our teaching practices and professional roles as teachers.

Pedagogical Activities

This series of pedagogical activities will assist you in relating to and making sense of the concepts that inform our understanding of *L2 learning as mediated and embodied*.

Experiencing

A. Language Socialization

Media such as books, videos, video games, movies, and televisions play a significant role in socializing children, adolescents, and adults into ways of understanding and making meaning in their social worlds. For each stage of your life (childhood, adolescence, and adulthood), choose two or three media that you feel have been the most influential to your development of your semiotic repertoire. For each medium, list specific ways – positive and negative – it has shaped specific registers comprising your repertoire. Create a visual representation of the paths your socialization has taken and compare to your classmates. Conclude the activity with a discussion of possible implications for L2 teaching and learning.

B. Mediational Means

Obtain a video of a classroom. Classbank is an open repository of videos that is located at talkbank.org. You can find a video there or you can search for one using an internet browser if you do not have a video available. As you view the video, identify and discuss at least four different mediational means that are being used. Then consider the following questions:

- What kinds of knowledge and skills are the students being socialized into?
- How does this context compare to your schooling contexts in terms of mediational means?
- What features are similar?
- What features are different?
- What can you conclude about the links between teaching and learning?

Conceptualizing

A. Concept Development

Select two of the concepts listed in Box 5.1. Craft a definition of each of the two concepts in your own words. Create one or two concrete examples of the concept that you have either experienced first-hand or can imagine. Pose one or two questions that you still have about the concept and develop a way to gather more information.

Box 5.1 Concepts: L2 learning is mediated and embodied

embodied resources　　　　language socialization
indexicality　　　　　　　　mediation
indexicals　　　　　　　　　mediational means

B. Concept Development

Choose one of the concepts you selected on which to gather additional information. Using the internet, search for information about the concept. Create a list of five or so facts about it. These can include names of scholars who study the concept, studies that have been done on the concept along with their findings, visual images depicting the concept, and so on. Create a concept web that visually records the information you gathered from your explorations.

Analyzing

A. Indexicals

Choose one of the commercials to view. Discuss the meanings that are being indexed in the semiotic resources that are used, e.g., linguistic constructions, prosodic cues, nonverbal behaviors such as facial expressions and gestures, artifacts etc.

1. This is a commercial for Bud Light, a beer. It consists of one word, "dude", being uttered in different situations.
   www.youtube.com/watch?v=3bFsqk84frI.
2. The next two are commercials for State Farm Insurance Company. Each depicts two difference scenes with the same dialogue.
   www.youtube.com/watch?v=LOjETlSufwo.
   www.youtube.com/watch?v=ultPAIkFoRw.

B. Embodied Resources

Choose one of the studies below on the embodied resources of L2 teaching and learning. Summarize the study, using the following questions to guide you:
- What is the purpose of the study?
- What are the main concepts?
- What methods and procedures for collecting and analyzing the data were used?
- What are the findings?
- What implications can you derive for understanding L2 teaching and learning?

1. Eskildsen, S. & Wagner, J. (2015). Embodied L2 construction learning. 65(2), *Language Learning*, 419–448.
2. Käänta, L. (2012) Teachers' embodied allocations in instructional interaction. *Classroom Discourse*, 3(2), 166–186.
3. Rosborough, A. (2014). Gesture, meaning-making, and embodiment: Second language learning in an elementary classroom. *Journal of Pedagogy*, (5), 227–250.
4. Cekaite, A. (2012). Affective stances in teacher-novice student interactions: Language, embodiment, and willingness to learn in a Swedish primary classroom. *Language in Society*, (41), 641–670.

Applying

A. Language Socialization

Create a multimodal project in which you document your professional socialization as an L2 teacher. Consider the people, the activities, and the semiotic resources that were most important along the way. Also consider the development of your beliefs such as those about teaching and your role as teacher, about the classroom, about students, about professional development and your professional vision, and so on.

B. Gestures as Mediational Means

Using one or two of the studies on the embodied resources of L2 teaching and learning as models, design a *single case study* in which you explore the role of gesture in teaching and learning. A single case study is an in-depth empirical examination of one specific person, group, or context. In the design, include the following information:

- Identification of the classroom and participants.
- Descriptions of the lesson or set of lessons on which you will collect data, how long you anticipate the lessons to be, and the means you

will use to collect the data. While there are many means for collecting data, for a study on the use of gesture, videotaping is the most comprehensive means.
- Identification of the means you will use to secure participants' consent, how you will arrange and manage the video recorders in the classroom, and any additional data you plan to collect.
- Description of how you will analyze the data.
- Anticipated implications for enhancing your understandings of the role of gesture in teaching and learning.

References

Baquedano-López, P., & Kattan, S. (2008). Language socialization in schools. In *Encyclopedia of language and education* (pp. 2729–2741). Springer US.

Belhiah, H. (2013). Using the hand to choreograph instruction: On the functional role of gesture in definition talk. *The Modern Language Journal*, 97(2), 417–434.

Byrnes, H. (2008). Advanced language learning: The contribution of Halliday and Vygotsky. New York; London: Continuum.

Christie, F. (2008). Genres and institutions: Functional perspectives on educational discourse. In M. Martin-Jones, A. M. de Mejia & N. Hornberger (Eds.), *Encyclopedia of language and education* (2nd ed., pp. 29–40). The Netherlands: Springer.

Christie, F., & Martin, J. R. (Eds.) (2007). Language, knowledge and pedagogy: Functional linguistic and sociological perspectives. London: Continuum.

Churchill, E., Okada, H., Nishino, T., & Atkinson, D. (2010). Symbiotic gesture and the sociocognitive visibility of grammar in second language acquisition. *The Modern Language Journal*, 94(2), 234–253.

Duff, P. A. (2007). Second language socialization as sociocultural theory: Insights and issues. *Language Teaching*, 40(4), 309–319.

Duff, P. A. (2008). Language socialization, higher education, and work. In N. Hornberger (Ed.), *Encyclopedia of language and education* (pp. 2818–2831). The Netherlands: Springer.

Duff, P. A. (2011). Second language socialization. In A. Duranti, E. Ochs & B. Schieffelin (Eds.), *The handbook of language socialization* (pp. 564–586). Oxford: Blackwell.

Duff, P. A., & May, S. (Eds.) (2017). *Language socialization*. The Netherlands: Springer.

Ellis, N. C., & Larsen–Freeman, D. (2006). Language emergence: Implications for applied linguistics. Introduction to the Special Issue. *Applied Linguistics*, 27, 558–589.

Ervin-Tripp, S., & Mitchell-Kernan, C. (Eds.) (1977). *Child discourse*. New York: Academic Press.

Eskildsen, S. W., & Wagner. J. (2013). Recurring and shared gestures in the L2 classroom: Resources for teaching and learning. *European Journal of Applied Linguistics*, 1(1), 1–23.

Eskildsen, S. W., & Wagner, J. (2015). Embodied L2 construction learning. *Language Learning*, 65(2), 268–297.

Hall, J. K. (2011). *Teaching and researching language and culture*, 2nd ed. London: Pearson.
Halliday, M. A. K. (1973). *Explorations in the functions of language*. London: Edward Arnold.
Halliday, M. A. K. (1978). *Language as social semiotic*. London: Edward Arnold.
Halliday, M. A. K. (1993). Toward a language-based theory of learning. *Linguistics and Education*, 5, 93–116.
Halliday, M. A. K. (1994). *An introduction to functional grammar*, 2nd ed. London: Arnold.
Hanks, W. F. (1999). Indexicality. *Journal of Linguistic Anthropology*, 9(1/2), 124–126.
Heath, S. B. (1983). Ways with words: Language, life, and work in communities and in classrooms. Cambridge: Cambridge University Press.
Hudson, N. (2011). Teacher gesture in a post-secondary English as a second language classroom: A sociocultural approach. Unpublished doctoral dissertation, University of Nevada, Las Vegas.
Hymes, D. (1962). The ethnography of speaking. In T. Gladwin & W. Sturtevant (Eds.), *Anthropology and human behavior* (pp. 15–53). Washington, DC: Anthropological Society of Washington.
Hymes, D. (1964). Formal discussion. The acquisition of language: Monographs of the society for research in child development, 29, 107–111.
Hymes, D. (1974). *Foundations in sociolinguistics: An ethnographic approach*. Philadelphia: University of Pennsylvania Press.
Lantolf, J. P. (Ed.) (2000). Second language learning as a mediated process. *Language Teaching*, 33, 79–96.
Lortie, D. (1975). *Schoolteacher: A sociological study*. London: University of Chicago Press.
Martin, J. R. (2006). Metadiscourse: Designing interaction in genre-based literacy programs. In R. Whittaker, M. O'Donnell & C. McCabe (Eds.), *Language and literacy: Functional approaches* (pp. 95–122). London: Continuum.
Martin, J. R. (2009). Genre and language learning: A social semiotic perspective. *Linguistics and Education*, 20, 10–21.
Matsumoto, Y., & Dobs, A. M. (2017). Pedagogical gestures as interactional resources for teaching and learning tense and aspect in the ESL grammar classroom. *Language Learning*, 67(1), 7–42.
Matthiessen, C. M. (2009). Meaning in the making: Meaning potential emerging from acts of meaning. *Language Learning*, 59(s1), 206–229.
Mondada, L. (2014). The local constitution of multimodal resources for social interaction. *Journal of Pragmatics*, 65, 137–156.
Mori, J., & Hayashi, M. (2006). The achievement of intersubjectivity through embodied completions: A study of interactions between first and second language speakers. *Applied Linguistics*, 27(2), 195–219.
Ochs, E. (1988). *Culture and language development: Language acquisition and language socialization in a Samoan village*. Cambridge: Cambridge University Press.
Ochs, E. (1996). Linguistic resources for socializing humanity. In J. J. Gumperz & S. Levinson (Eds.), *Rethinking linguistic relativity* (pp. 407–437), Cambridge: Cambridge University Press.

Ochs, E., & Schieffelin, B. B. (1984). Language acquisition and socialization: Three developmental stories. In R. A. Shweder & R. A. LeVine (Eds.), *Culture theory: Essays on mind, self, and emotion* (pp. 276–320). Cambridge: Cambridge University Press.
Ochs, E., & Schieffelin, B. B. (2008). "Language socialization: An historical overview". *Encyclopedia of Language and Education, Volume 8: Research Methods in Language and Education* (pp. 3–16). The Netherlands: Kluwer Academic Publishers.
Ochs, E., & Schieffelin, B. (2017). Language socialization: An historical overview. In A. Duranti, E. Ochs & B. Schieffelin (Eds.), *Language socialization* (pp. 3–16). The Netherlands: Springer, Cham.
Olsher, D. (2004). Talk and gesture: The embodied completion of sequential actions in spoken interaction. In R. Gardner & J. Wagner (Eds.), *Second language conversations* (pp. 221–246). London: Continuum.
Schieffelin, B. B., & Ochs, E. (1986). Language socialization. *Annual Review of Anthropology*, 15(1), 163–191.
Slobin, D. (1967). *A field manual for cross-cultural study of the acquisition of communicative competence.* Berkeley: University of California.
Slobin, D. (Ed.) (1985). *A cross-linguistic study of language acquisition* (vols. 1–2). Hillsdale, NJ: Erlbaum.
Smotrova, T., & Lantolf, J. P. (2013). The function of gesture in lexically focused L2 instructional conversations. *The Modern Language Journal*, 97(2), 397–416.
Tomasello, M. (2003). *Constructing a language: A usage-based theory of language acquisition.* Cambridge, MA: Harvard University Press.
Tomasello, M. (2008). *Origins of human cognition.* Cambridge, MA: MIT Press.
van Compernolle, R. A., & Smotrova, T. (2014). Corrective feedback, gesture, and mediation in classroom language learning. *Language and Sociocultural Theory*, 1(1), 25–47.
van Compernolle, R. A., & Williams, L. (2011). Thinking with your hands: Speech–gesture activity during an L2 awareness-raising task. *Language Awareness*, 20(3), 203–219.
Vygotsky, L. S. (1978). *Mind in society.* Cambridge, MA: Harvard University Press.
Vygotsky, L. S. (1981). The genesis of higher mental functions. In J. V. Wertsch (Ed.), *The concept of activity in soviet psychology* (pp. 144–188). Armonk, NY: M. E. Sharpe.
Vygotsky, L. S. (1987). *The collected works of LS Vygotsky: Volume 1: Problems of general psychology* (Vol. 1). Springer Science & Business Media.
Vygotsky, L. S. (1989). Concrete human psychology. *Soviet psychology*, 27(2), 53–77.
Vygotsky, L. S. (1994). The problem of the environment. In R. van der Veer & J. Valsiner (Eds.), *The Vygotsky reader* (pp. 338–354). Oxford: Blackwell.
Williams, R. (1977). *Marxism and literature* (Vol. 1). Oxford: Oxford Paperbacks.
Wertsch, J. V. (1994). The primacy of mediated action in sociocultural studies. *Mind, Culture, and Activity*, 1(4), 202–208.

Chapter 6
L2 Learning Is Mediated by Learners' Social Identities

Overview

At the meso level of social activity are the sociocultural institutions within which contexts of interaction are situated. These institutions include the family, neighborhoods, schools, and places of work and worship. Also included are social and community organizations such as clubs, sports leagues, political parties, various online contexts, and so on. When L2 learners participate in particular social contexts of action of their social institutions, they do so as actors with specific constellations of historically laden, context-sensitive, and locally (re)produced social identities. In this chapter, we discuss the role that learners' identities play in mediating the development of L2 learners' repertoires of semiotic resources.

Social Identity

When we use our semiotic resources, we do so as individuals with multiple, dynamic, *social identities*. One facet of our identities is defined by macro-level demographic categories that are linked to the social groups into which we are born. These categories include social class, gender, race, ethnicity, religion, nationality, mother tongue(s), and generation. These have been referred to as *transportable identities* as, for the most part, these identities stay with us as we move across situations (Zimmerman, 1998).

For example, we are all born into families of particular socio-economic classes such as poor, working class, middle class, or prosperous and our memberships in these classes become part of our identities. Likewise, we are born into families who speak particular languages and thus take on identities as speakers of English, Chinese, Arabic, and so on. The geographical region in which we are born also provides us with particular group memberships and upon our birth we assume specific identities associated with nations and continents. We become identified as Canadian, British, African, South East Asian, and so on. Within national boundaries, we are defined by membership in regional groups, and we take on identities such as northerners, mid-westerners, or southerners and as city people, suburbanites, or rural residents. Finally, even the time period or generation into which we are born provides us with a particular identity. We become identified as Baby Boomers, Generation X-ers, Millennials, and so on.

A second dimension of our social identities is defined by the social roles and role relationships that are ascribed to us through our involvement in the various activities of the social institutions, such as school, church, family, and the workplace, comprising our communities. These institutions give shape to the kinds of social groups to which we have access and to the role-relationships we can establish with others. These have been referred to as *situated identities* (Zimmerman, 1998) and *role-relational identities* (Gee, 2017). For example, in schools, we take on roles such as teachers, students, or members of the administrative staff and in these roles, we assume particular relationships with others, such as student-teacher, student-student, teacher-teacher, teacher-administrative staff, and so on. Likewise, in our workplace, we assume roles as supervisors, managers, colleagues, or subordinates.

Another component of our situated identities is defined by the activities in which we are involved. Gee (2017) refers to these as *activity-based identities*. These are freely chosen identities, are wide ranging and include, for example, gamers, birders, carpenters, writers, gardeners, social activists, sports fans, and so on. Gee explains,

> Activity-based identities are another form of collective intelligence, perhaps the most important form in today's world. When someone takes on – as master, adept or lay person – an activity-based identity, they are networked to the values, norms, practices, and shared knowledge and skills – as well as the smart tools and other resources – of a large group of people who, through time and space, develop and continually transform effective ways to do certain things and solve certain sorts of problems.
>
> (p. 85)

The ways we use our semiotic resources to enact our social identities are not based solely on personal intentions. Rather, our identities embody particular histories of expectations that have been developed over time by other group members enacting similar roles in the various contexts of action of their social institutions. These include expectations about particular registers for enacting our identities, beliefs, and attitudes about the kinds of groups to which we have access and the role-relationships we can establish with others.

Our social identities, then, afford us access to particular activities and to particular role-defined relationships with others. For example, depending on where a person is born, the opportunities for group identification including access to particular activities and resources, will vary depending on a person's gender, race, social class, and so on. Opportunities for a white male born into a working-class family in a rural area in the northwest region of the United States, for example, will differ from those of a white male born into an upper-class family in the same area.

Our role relational identities are intimately linked to our transportable identities in that the expectations we hold about ours and others' roles and role relationships are tied to ours and others' transportable identities. For example, we tend to associate certain roles with particular transportable identities. In some groups, women are more often associated with care-giving roles such as teacher, nurse, and social worker, while men are usually associated with administrative roles such as executive, manager, and school principal. Associating transportable identities with particular roles can make it difficult for us to perform roles that are not conventionally linked to our identities. In some groups, a female taking on the role of chief executive in a business may experience difficulties in performing satisfactorily if the role is conventionally associated with males (Tracy & Robles, 2013).

We approach our activities with the expectations we have come to associate with ours and others' social identities, and we use them to make sense of each other's involvement in our encounters. Our expectations about what we can and cannot do as members of our various social groups are built up over time through socialization into our own social groups. The semiotic resources we use to communicate, and our interpretations of those used by others, are shaped by these mutually held expectations. Richard Bauman explains the inextricable link between social identity and semiotic resources in Quote 6.1.

Quote 6.1 Social Identity and Semiotic Resources

[Social identity] is the situated outcome of a rhetorical and interpretive process in which interactants make situationally motivated selections from socially constituted repertoires of identificational and affiliational resources and craft these semiotic resources into identity claims for presentation to others.

Bauman (2000, p. 1)

Our identities are not fixed or static but are fluid and "multifaceted in complex and contradictory ways" (Miller, 2000, p. 72) and reflective of the landscapes of our lived experiences (Wenger, 2010). Moreover, we never enact just one identity at a time. Rather, we have a nexus of memberships, which are in complex relation to each other, and constantly shifting and evolving across time and space (Douglas Fir Group, 2016; Ochs, 1993). In every act of meaning making, one or more of our social identities are "inferred and interactionally achieved" (Ochs, 1993, p. 291) through the simultaneous deployment of multiple semiotic resources, such as words, prosodic cues, gestures, facial expressions, and other resources that are associated with specific social groups (Bucholtz & Hall, 2005).

As mentioned previously, how we enact our identities depends on our expectations about our own identities and those of others. However, while our expectations influence our actions, they do not determine them. At any moment, there exists the possibility of taking up a unique stance towards our own identity and those of others, and of using our semiotic resources in unexpected ways towards unexpected goals (Hall, 2011; Norton & McKinney, 2011; Toohey, Day, & Manyak, 2007).

Social Identity and L2 Learning

The study of the mediating role that L2 learners' social identities play in learners' success in negotiating their access to and participation in various L2 social activities and groups has been the concern of a growing body of research in SLA. One early influential study is that by Bonny Norton (Norton, 2000; Pierce, 1995). Drawing on poststructuralist theory, and in particular the work of Weedon (1997) and Bourdieu (1991), Norton examined how the identities of a group of women who had migrated to Canada from different regions of the world were differentially constructed in their interactions with others in and out of the classroom. She argues that these different constructions had a significant influence on the women's interest in language learning, making some more willing than others to invest the time and effort needed to learn English.

Norton's study set off a ground swell of interest in the study of various types of identity and language learning. Some have examined how learners' identities *as* learners are constructed (e.g., Cekaite & Evaldsson, 2008; Dagenais, Day, & Toohey, 2006; Song, 2010; Toohey, 2000). The study by McKay and Wong (1996), for example, examines how four Mandarin-speaking adolescents attempted to negotiate the shaping of their identities as English language learners and users in the contexts of their schools, and the consequences of their attempts relative to the development of their academic skills in English. Additional studies have similarly focused on how L2 learners negotiate their identities as learners and users of the L2. For example, the study by Daganeis, Day, and Toohey (2006), reveal how differences in literacy practices to which a multilingual child was given access in her French immersion classroom mediated teacher expectations of her future educational progress as an English language learner. Two of her teachers saw her as a capable learner while another teacher constructed her as a weak learner whose English skills needed remediation.

Also examined has been the role that learners' gender identities play in mediating L2 learners' learning trajectories (e.g., Hruska, 2004; Menard-Warwick, 2009; Morita, 2009; Skilton-Sylvester, 2002). For example, in her longitudinal study of four Cambodian women studying English in an adult community center in the United States, Skilton-Sylvester (2002) found that the ways that the women's identities as spouses, mothers, sisters, daughters, and workers were addressed in the class influenced their participation. For two women, their roles as wives directly impacted their participation in their ESL program. One's identity as an English learner was supported by her husband and she progressed quickly in the class. Another student's identity was perceived as a threat to her husband, leading her to stop attending classes because she was "unable to maintain her identity as a student alongside her identity as a wife" (ibid, p. 17). Morita's (2009) study showed how a male student could also feel alienated from learning opportunities. In this case, the individual was a PhD student in a Canadian university who felt marginalized because his theoretical perspective did not align with the disciplinary discourse of his academic department where feminism and critical theories were popular perspectives.

It is not the case that one's gender identity only constrains L2 learning. As Miller and Kubota (2013) point out, enhanced and empowered gender identities can be associated with learning a language. This is exemplified in Pavlenko's (2001) study of L2 learners' memoirs, in which she found that for some female writers, the process of learning another language was perceived positively as a "reinvention of self through friendship and as connectedness with others" (p. 229).

Relationships between learners' racial identities and L2 learning have also been explored by scholars (Ibrahim, 1999; Lin et al., 2004; Curtis & Romney, 2006; McKinney, 2007; Kubota & Lin, 2009; Shin, 2012, 2015). One early study by Ibrahim (1999) investigated how race impacted the L2 learning opportunities of immigrant African students in a Canadian high school. Ibrahim found that the students appropriated a nonmainstream language, African American English, as their L2 and in so doing created a particular identity of being black that was familiar to and respected by their peers. Shin (2012) examined how race and ethnicity intersected in the emergence of a new identity for Korean students in Canada. These students were what Shin labeled "yuhaksaeng", i.e., Korean nationals with student visas. She found that, despite investing heavily in learning English, their investment did not succeed as in their local community of English speakers they were ascribed identities not as global cosmopolitans, but as fresh-off-the-boat Korean immigrants. To resist this racial marginalization, the students claimed a new identity that was "simultaneously global and Korean" (p. 185). They did so by mobilizing varieties of their Korean language and culture to construct themselves as "wealthy, modern, and cosmopolitan 'Cools' *vis-á-vis* both long-term immigrants in local Korean diasporic communities and '[White] Canadians'" (ibid.).

More recently, Darvin and Norton (2014) have argued for the need to include social class as a mediating factor of L2 learners' opportunities for learning, claiming that social class differences in transnational contexts can impact L2 learners' social and educational trajectories. They support their claim with a case study investigating the different opportunities to learn English afforded to adolescent migrant students residing in Canada. Both students came from the same country but their paths to Canada differed. One student, Ayrton, came from a well-to-do family that immigrated to Canada through a program designed to attract business people with substantial financial capital. In Canada, he attended a private school. The other student, John, came from a working-class family. His mother had been working in Canada for six years as a caregiver and John immigrated through a program that allowed his mother to apply for permanent residency for him in Canada. In his new community, John attended an inner-city public school. These class differences afforded Ayrton and John different opportunities to increase their economic, cultural, and social capital as immigrants in Canada. Ayrton was able to build greater capital while John's opportunities remained limited. Darvin and Norton conclude that studies of identity and L2 learning must include social class as a significant variable in understanding the varied educational and social trajectories of L2 learners.

Another aspect of L2 learners' social identities that shapes their L2 learning opportunities is their *imagined identity* as part of memberships in *imagined communities* (Kanno & Norton, 2003; Norton & Toohey, 2011; Pavlenko & Norton, 2007). Imagined communities are "groups of people, not immediately tangible and accessible, with whom we connect through the power of the imagination" (Kanno & Norton, 2003, p. 241). L2 learners desire to become members of imagined communities because they perceive that the communities can offer them opportunities to expand their range of identities and to increase their access to social, educational, and financial resources. L2 learners' imagined identities in their imagined communities can push them to seek out and pursue L2 learning opportunities that might not otherwise be available to them. Such was the case, for example, for a group of immigrant parents of diverse language origins residing in Canada. This group of parents chose to enroll their children in French immersion programs so that they would be better equipped to take on identities as English–French bilinguals and thereby have access to economically more powerful contexts of interaction within their desired social institutions (Dagenais, 2003).

It is not always the case that real communities meet the expectations of learners' imagined communities and identities. This was the case for a Japanese teenager, as reported by Kanno and Norton (2003). Although the student spent two thirds of his life in the English-speaking countries of Australia and Canada, he held firmly to his identity as Japanese and made every effort to maintain his Japanese language. However, upon his return to Japan, he found that his imagined community bore little resemblance to the "real" Japan, a discovery which led to his rejection of his Japanese identity. Differences between real and imagined communities can be even more consequential to L2 learners if access to their imagined communities is blocked or marginalized by the very people with whom they aspire to interact (Norton, 2001). This can lead to withdrawal from the community, and loss of desire to continue to learn the language of the community.

Digital Communication and Changing Identities

The expansion of digital technologies and social networking sites has created new transnational, online social spaces, which have become increasingly important arenas for the development and display of multiple activity-based identities, such as bloggers, gamers, web designers, fanfiction writers, and readers (Chen, 2013; Darvin, 2016; Duff, 2015; Lam, 2004, 2009; Thorne & Black, 2011; Thorne, Suaro, & Smith, 2015). These spaces and identities afford L2 learners multiple and varied opportunities to connect with others who share these interests.

Thorne and Black's (2011) case study of an English language learner's participation in an online fan fiction site illustrates this point. In their study, they show how joining a fanfiction site afforded Nanako, an English language learner from China and residing in a large city in Canada, opportunities to transform her identity as a writer. When Nanako first joined the site, in her representations of self to others, she positioned herself as inexperienced, not just with English, but as a writer of fan fiction as well. Over time, two dynamics led to a repositioning of her identity. One dynamic was the extensive opportunities to interact with a diverse group of fans from around the world who shared interests. This increased her confidence in her writing, and thus reshaped her position within the community to successful author. The second dynamic was the realization that her identity as a speaker of Chinese and her knowledge of Asian languages and cultures were valuable resources for her fanfiction texts. This realization helped her reposition herself as an expert. Thorne and Black conclude that such digital spaces can offer L2 learners a wide range of possibilities "for self-representation and the construction of identities as capable users of multiple social languages" (ibid., p. 276).

Summary

L2 learners inhabit multiple, intersecting social identities, both real and imagined, which are significant to the development of their semiotic repertoires in that they mediate in important ways learners' access to their opportunities for language learning. Depending on transportable identities such as gender, race, and social class, situated identities such as learners and spouses, and activity-based identities such as gamers and fanfiction writers, L2 learners may find that the opportunities they have access to are abundant and boundless in some cases, and limited or constrained in others. Digital technologies have expanded possibilities for L2 learning by creating new transnational spaces that afford new identity possibilities. In these worlds, L2 learners are able to perform different, activity-based identities through "creative assembly, aligning themselves with different communities and imagining other identities" (Darvin, 2016, p. 536).

Implications for Understanding L2 Teaching

At the meso level of social activity, L2 learning is mediated by learners' varied social identities. From an understanding of the inextricable links between social identity and the development of learners' communicative repertoires, we can derive four implications for understanding L2 teaching.

1   L2 learners typically enter our classrooms with institutionally ascribed learner identities such as "good" or "struggling", "hardworking" or "apathetic", as defined by institutional standards. Taking into consideration only these institutional identities renders invisible the fact that students participate in our learning environments from multiple, complex, and sometime conflicting, identity positions. Our teaching practices cannot ignore these identities but, instead, must treat them as primary resources for teaching and learning. In our practices, we must provide learners with a range of diverse opportunities and positions from which to engage in learning the L2. Our teaching practices must not only help learners recognize how their varied identities mediate their learning both in and out of the classroom; they must also provide them with strategies and practices for drawing on and transforming their identities in ways that positively impact their engagement in learning.

2   As important to our learners' experiences in the classroom are their imagined identities and communities. Together with our learners, we must explore the identities and communities that are both desirable and possible for them. We must be mindful, however, that any unspoken beliefs we may have about learners' possibilities do not constrain our explorations. In designing our learning environments, we must take students' imagined identities into consideration to ensure that the learning is meaningful and relevant; we need to design practices that connect learners' aspirations to particular registers for realizing their imagined identities and facilitate the expansion of their repertoires. While recognizing the positive potential that incorporating learners' imagined identities can have for L2 learning, we must also be mindful that L2 teachers should not assume

> the authority to define and assign possible imagined identities for their language learners, nor should they treat them as tabula rasa with regard to students' life experience. Teachers should remember the limits of their professional and personal influence on their learners, for educators enter the life of students only at some particular point, but the learning experience also happened before and will continue in the future; the most important thing for [L2] teachers is not to discourage their learners' desire to acquire some new identities.
>
> (Kharchenko, 2014, p. 36)

3   We, as teachers, also bring multiple complex identities to our classrooms. How our learners perceive us – our gender, social class, nationality, our roles as academics, spouses, parents etc. – shapes their expectations of us, their interactions with us, and, more generally, their experiences in our classrooms. Teachers who understand their own identities and both the opportunities and constraints they make possible in terms of their relationships with students can use their understandings to develop teaching practices that build relationships with their students, which, in turn, can significantly heighten students' engagement in their learning contexts.

4   Digital technologies and social networking sites will continue to expand possibilities for activity-based identity construction and community participation for our L2 learners. We need to reimagine the role that our classrooms can play in linking learners to these virtual worlds and enhancing their ability to be "semiotically agile and adept across communicative modalities" (Thorne, Sauro, & Black, 2015, p. 229). While we do not have to be experts in these technologies and virtual social worlds, we must be cognizant of their affordances and able to design contexts of learning that facilitate our learners' participation and expansion of their semiotic repertoires.

Pedagogical Activities

This series of pedagogical activities will assist you in relating to and making sense of the concepts that inform our understanding of *L2 learning as mediated by learners' social identities*.

Experiencing

A. Social Identities

Create a diagram using, for example, an identity chart or wheel (or other type of diagram) of what you consider to be your most significant transportable, situated, and activity-based identities. Figure 6.1 is an example of an identity chart. For each identity, note a few types of learning experiences that the identity affords and a few types that it constrains. Compare your representations with those of your classmates and consider the following questions:

- What are the similarities, what are the differences?
- What conclusions can you draw about social identity and your own learning experiences?

B. Language Teacher Identities

Describe yourself in terms of your teacher identities. If you are not yet a teacher, describe your imagined teacher identities. Then, consider the following quote. First, restate it in your own words and then discuss it in terms of your own professional identity development. Relate it to experiences you have had or can imagine having. What implications are there for your future as an L2 teacher?

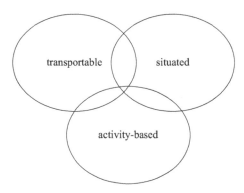

Figure 6.1 Identity chart.

104   Learners' Social Identities

the negotiation of teachers' professional identities is... powerfully influenced by contextual factors outside of the teachers themselves and their preservice education.... [T]he identity resources of the teachers may be tested against conditions that challenge and conflict with their backgrounds, skills, social memberships, use of language, beliefs, values, knowledge, attitudes, and so on. Negotiating those challenges forms part of the dynamic of professional identity development.

(Miller, 2009, p. 175)

Conceptualizing

A. Concept Development

Select two of the concepts listed in Box 6.1. Craft a definition of each of the two concepts in your own words. Create one or two concrete examples of the concept that you have either experienced first-hand or can imagine. Pose one or two questions that you still have about the concept and develop a way to gather more information.

Box 6.1 Concepts: L2 learning is mediated by learners' social identities

activity-based identities   situated identities
imagined communities   social identities
imagined identities   transportable identities

B. Concept Development

Choose one of the concepts you selected from the list on which to gather additional information. Using the internet, search for information on the concept. Create a list of five or so facts about it. These can include names of scholars who study the concept, studies that have been done on the concept along with their findings, visual images depicting the concept, and so on. Create a concept web that visually records the information you gathered from your explorations.

Analyzing

A. Social Identity and L2 Learning

Choose one of the following memoirs, in which the author recounts his/her experiences learning an additional language. After reading the book, write an essay in which you address the following questions.

- What events in the author's life does the memoir focus on?
- How does the author position him/herself relative to the language being learned?
- What identities seem to play a role in how the author positions him/herself and how the author is positioned by others?
- What conclusions can you draw about social identity and L2 learning?

1 William Alexander (2014). Flirting with French: How a language charmed me, seduced me, and nearly broke my heart.
2 Deborah Fallows (2011). Dreaming in Chinese: Mandarin lessons in life, love, and language.
3 Katherine Russell Rich (2009). Dreaming in Hindi: Coming awake in another language.
4 Ilan Stavans (2002). On borrowed words: A memoir of language.
5 Dianne Hales (2009). La Bella Lingua: My love affair with Italian, the world's most enchanting language.

B. Social Identity and L2 Learning

With a partner or group members, conduct a small study on social identity and L2 learning in which you interview a group of adult L2 learners on their experiences learning another language. First, choose a group of learners you are interested in discovering more about and seek their consent to participate. You may also be required to seek approval from your institutional human subject review board. Develop a set of open-ended questions on the topic for the interview. Record each interview (be sure the equipment works well beforehand!) and transcribe the recordings. Content analysis is a useful technique for systematically analyzing such data. Read through the set of interviews first. Next, define your categories, e.g., types of identities, types of L2 learning experiences, and so on. Reread the interviews, and mark keywords and phrases that correspond to the categories. Interpret your findings and report them in a multimodal text to be shared with others. For assistance in conducting a content analysis, conduct a search for materials using an internet browser.

Applying

A. Social Identity

Create a multimodal memoir that recounts how a significant experience or experiences in your trajectory as an additional language learner (re)shaped aspects of your social identities and/or led to the development of new identities. Share with your classmates and/or others by publishing on a shared platform.

B. Digital Communities and Activity-Based Identities

Choose two or three online communities and/or social networking sites in which you regularly participate. Create a multimodal text in which you 1. describe each site and the different types of activity-based identities the site affords you and 2. reflect on the role(s) that your participation in these digital spaces plays in (re)shaping your registers and your identities. Consider two or three ways you can draw on your experiences in your online worlds to apply to the work you do as an L2 teacher.

References

Bauman, R. (2000). Language, identity, performance. *Pragmatics, 10*(1), 1–5.
Bourdieu, P. (1991). *Language and symbolic power.* Oxford: Polity.
Bucholtz, M., & Hall, K. (2005). Identity and interaction: A sociocultural linguistic approach. *Discourse Studies, 7*(4–5), 585–614.
Cekaite, A., & Evaldsson, A.-C. (2008). Staging linguistic identities and negotiating monolingual norms in multiethnic school settings. *International Journal of Multilingualism, 5*(3), 177–196.
Chen, H. (2013). Identity practices of multilingual writers in social networking spaces. *Language Learning & Technology, 17*(2), 143–170.
Curtis, A., & M. Romney (2006). *Color, race, and English language teaching: Shades of meaning.* Mahwah, NJ: Lawrence Erlbaum.
Dagenais, D. (2003). Accessing imagined communities through multilingualism and immersion education. Special issue of *Language, Identity and Education, 2,* 269–283.
Dagenais, D., Toohey, K., & Day, E. (2006). A multilingual child's literacy practices and contrasting identities in the figured worlds of French immersion classrooms. *International Journal of Bilingual Education and Bilingualism, 9,* 205–218.
Darvin, R. (2016). Language and identity in the digital age. In R. Darvin & S. Preece (Eds.), *Routledge handbook of language and identity* (pp. 523–540). Oxford: Routledge.
Darvin, R., & Norton, B. (2014). Social class, identity, and migrant students. *Journal of Language, Identity & Education, 13*(2), 111–117.
Douglas Fir Group (2016). A transdisciplinary framework for SLA in a multilingual world. *The Modern Language Journal, 100,* 19–47.
Duff, P. A. (2015). Transnationalism, multilingualism, and identity. *Annual Review of Applied Linguistics, 35,* 57–80.
Gee, J. P. (2017). Identity and diversity in today's world. *Multicultural Education Review, 9*(2), 83–92.
Hall, J. K. (2011). *Teaching and researching language and culture,* 2nd ed. London: Person.
Hruska, B. L. (2004). Constructing gender in an English dominant kindergarten: Implications for second language learners. *TESOL Quarterly, 38*(3), 459.
Ibrahim, A. E. K. M. (1999). Becoming Black: Rap and hip-hop, race, gender, identity, and the politics of ESL learning. *TESOL Quarterly, 33*(3), 349–369.

Kanno, Y., & Norton, B. (2003). Imagined communities and educational possibilities. *Journal of Language, Identity, and Education.* Special issue on. 2(4), 241–249.

Kharchenko, N. (2014). Imagined communities and teaching English as a second language. *Journal of Foreign Languages*, 2(1), 21–39.

Kubota, R., & Lin, A. (2006). Race and TESOL: Introduction to concepts and theories. *TESOL Quarterly, 40*(3), 471–493.

Lam, W. S. E. (2004). Second language socialization in a bilingual chatroom. *Language Learning & Technology, 8,* 44–65.

Lam, W. S. E. (2009). Multiliteracies on instant messaging in negotiating local, translocal, and transnational affiliations: A case of an adolescent immigrant. *Reading Research Quarterly, 44*(4), 377–397.

Lin, A., R. Grant, R. Kubota, S. Motha, G. Tinker Sachs, & Vandrick, S. (2004). Women faculty of color in TESOL: Theorizing our lived experiences. *TESOL Quarterly, 38*(3), 487–504.

McKay, S. L., & Wong, S.-L. C. (1996). Multiple discourses, multiple identities: Investment and agency in second-language learning among Chinese adolescent immigrant students. *Harvard Educational Review, 66,* 577–608.

McKinney, C. (2007). "If I speak English does it make me less black anyway?" "Race" and English in South African desegregated schools. *English Academy Review, 24*(2), 6–24.

Menard-Warwick, J. (2009). *Gendered identities and immigrant language learning.* Clevedon: Multilingual Matters.

Miller, E., & Kubota, R. (2013). Second language identity construction. In J. Herschensohn & M. Young-Scholten (Eds.), *The Cambridge handbook of second language acquisition* (pp. 230–250). New York: Cambridge University Press.

Miller, J. (2009). Teacher identity. In A. E. Burns & J. C. Richards (Eds.), *The Cambridge guide to second language teacher education* (pp. 172–181). New York: Cambridge University Press.

Miller, J. M. (2000). Language use, identity, and social interaction: Migrant students in Australia. *Research on language and social interaction, 33*(1), 69–100.

Morita, N. (2009). Language, culture, gender, and academic socialization. *Language and Education, 23*(5), 443–460.

Norton, B. (2000). *Identity and language learning.* Harlow: Pearson Education

Norton, B. (2001). Non-participation, imagined communities, and the language classroom. In M. Breen (Ed.), *Learner contributions to language learning: New directions in research* (pp. 159–171). Harlow: Pearson Education.

Norton, B., & McKinney, C. (2011). Identity and second language acquisition. In D. Atkinson (Ed.), *Alternative approaches to second language acquisition* (pp. 73–94). New York: Routledge.

Norton, B., & Toohey, K. (2011). Identity, language learning, and social change. *Language Teaching, 44,* 412–446.

Ochs, E. (1993). Constructing social identity. *Research on Language and Social Interaction, 26,* 287–306.

Pavlenko, A. (2001). Language learning memoirs as a gendered genre. *Applied linguistics, 22*(2), 213–240.

Pavlenko, A., & Norton, B. (2007). Imagined communities, identity, and English language teaching. In J. Cummins & C. Davison (Eds.), *International handbook of English language teaching* (pp. 669–680). New York: Springer.

Pierce, B. N. (1995). Social identity, investment and language learning. *TESOL Quarterly, 29*, 9–31.

Shin, H. (2012). From FOB to cool: Transnational migrant students in Toronto and the styling of global linguistic capital. *Journal of Sociolinguistics, 16*(2), 184–200.

Shin, H. (2015). Everyday racism in Canadian schools: Ideologies of language and culture among Korean transnational students in Toronto. *Journal of Multilingual and Multicultural Development, 36*(1), 67–79.

Skilton-Sylvester, E. (2002). Should I stay or should I go? Investigating Cambodian women's participation and investment in adult ESL programs. *Adult Education Quarterly, 53*(1), 9–26.

Song, J. (2010). Language ideology and identity in transnational space: Globalization, migration, and bilingualism among Korean families in the USA. *International Journal of Bilingual Education and Bilingualism, 13*(1), 23–42.

Thorne, S. L., & Black, R. W. (2011). Identity and interaction in internet-mediated contexts. In C. Higgins (Ed.), *Identity formation in globalizing contexts* (pp. 257–278). De Gruyter.

Thorne, S. L., Sauro, S., & Smith, B. (2015). Technologies, identities, and expressive activity. *Annual Review of Applied Linguistics, 35*, 215–233.

Toohey, K. (2000). *Learning English at school: Identity, social relations, and classroom practice*. Clevedon: Multilingual Matters.

Toohey, K., Day, E., & Manyak, P. (2007). ESL learners in the early school years. In J. Cummins & C. Davison (Eds.), *International handbook of English language teaching* (pp. 625–638). Boston: Springer.

Tracy, K. & Robles, J. (2013). *Everyday talk: Building and reflecting identities*, 2nd ed. New York: Guilford Press.

Weedon, C. (1997). *Feminist practice and poststructuralist theory*, 2nd ed. Oxford: Blackwell.

Wenger, E. (2010). Communities of practice and social learning systems: The career of a concept. In C. Blackmore (Ed.), *Social learning systems and communities of practice* (pp. 179–198). London: Springer.

Zimmerman, D. H. (1998). Identity, context and interaction. In C. Antaki & S. Widdicombe (Eds.), *Identities in talk* (pp. 87–106). Thousand Oaks, CA: Sage.

Chapter 7

L2 Learning Is Mediated by Motivation, Investment, and Agency

Overview

As we discussed in Chapter 6, significant to the development of L2 learners' semiotic repertoires are their multiple, intersecting social identities. They draw on their understandings of their identities and those of others to negotiate their participation in their social activities. However, while their social identities influence their actions, they do not determine them. Also mediating their involvement at the meso level of social activity are their motivations for participating in their learning environments, their investments in their contexts of learning, both real and imagined, and their agentive capacities to act. In this chapter, we examine more closely how the constructs of motivation, investment and agency mediate L2 learning.

Motivation

One of the most researched constructs in SLA, motivation has been considered a key variable in explaining success in L2 learning. Early research operationalized motivation as a static individual trait, intrinsic to the learner. As understandings of language and learning have changed, so have understandings of motivation. Current understandings view it not as an individual attribute, but as an organic, dynamic construct that is continuously evolving from the interrelations between individuals and their social contexts (Ushioda & Dörnyei, 2009; Al-Hoorie, 2017).

Recall in Chapter 4 we discussed the motivational role that the interactional instinct plays in language learning. The interactional instinct is an innate drive that pushes individuals to seek out emotionally rewarding relationships with others (Lee et al., 2009; Schumann, 2010). As we noted, the older L2 learners are, the more complicated social relationships become and the less intense the reward may be that is derived from such relationships. Consequently, their motivation for seeking out opportunities to use the L2 in interactions with others may also be reduced.

However, as research has shown, there are other motivating factors in addition to forming relationships with speakers of the L2 such as enjoyment of the learning environment, and educational and economic aspirations. The study by Richards (2006) provides an example of how enjoyment of the learning environment can increase students' motivation. In his study, he showed how when different identities other than teacher and student were made relevant in classroom interactions, the student were more motivated to participate in their classroom activities. Their motivation was displayed in their increased involvement in the interactions and, more specifically, in their apparent willingness to volunteer information, respond to each other's turns with heightened excitement, and provide help where needed. Likewise, Dobs (2016) found that moments of shared laughter between a teacher and students increased students' motivation to participate in the class discussions, as displayed in a sustained increase in self-selected turns by the students. As a final example, the study by Henry, Davydenko, and Dörnyei (2015) of unusually successful adult migrant learners of Swedish found that the learners' positive evaluations of their imagined new identities and life experiences in their new home sustained powerful motivational behaviors for learning Swedish.

To capture the complex dimensions of motivation, Zoltan Dörnyei proposed the *L2 motivational self system* (Dörnyei, 2009; Ryan & Dörnyei, 2013). The system has three components, each which influences individuals' levels of motivation. The first two, the *ideal L2 self* and the *ought-to L2 self*, are related to self-image. The ideal L2 self has to do with the person one wants to be as an L2 user. The ought-to L2 self has to do with qualities one believes one should have to meet expectations and avoid negative consequences. The two types of selves are presumed to be powerful motivators for learners to succeed in learning other languages because of the psychological desire to reduce the discrepancy between one's actual and ideal selves. The third component of the L2 motivational self system is the L2 learning experience. This is concerned with the learning environment and includes factors related to the curriculum, the teacher, and instructional activities. A key component of the L2 motivational self system is vision, which is considered "one of the highest-order motivational forces" (Dörnyei & Kubanyiova, 2014, p. 9).

According to Dörnyei (2009), the import of the L2 motivational self system is that it suggests new avenues for motivating language learners. In particular, learners' desire to bridge the gap between the actual self and future self has been shown to be an effective motivator if learners have visions of their future selves that are elaborate and vivid and are in harmony with the expectations of the learners' social environments.

A key strategy is helping learners to create their visions of their ideal selves. This entails "increasing the students' mindfulness about the significance of ideal selves, guiding them through a number of possible selves that they have entertained in their minds in the past, and presenting powerful role models" (Dörnyei, 2009, p. 33).

Building on the framework for vision of possible selves and its link to learners' motivation offered by the L2 motivational system, more recently Dörnyei and his colleagues developed the construct of *directed motivational current* (DMC) (Dörnyei, Muir, & Ibrahim, 2014; Dörnyei, Ibrahim, & Muir, 2015; Muir & Dörnyei, 2013). A DMC is "an intense motivational drive which is capable of both stimulating and supporting long-term behaviour, such as learning a foreign/second language (L2)" (Dörnyei, Muir, & Ibrahim, 2014, p. 9).

DMCs have several characteristics. First, they are goal and vision oriented. A vision involves tangible images related to achieving the goal. Second, DMCs have a recognizable structure in that there is a clear starting point and behavioral routines related to the accomplishment of the goal. Third, people with DMCs have complete ownership of the process and confidence in their abilities to achieve their goals. Fourth, people experience highly positive emotions toward the process as they progress toward their goals. DMCs are rewarding because they propel the individual in the direction of a personally satisfying, highly valued goal or vision through goal-oriented action. Dörnyei, Ibrahim and Muir (2015) provide examples of DMCs in educational settings in Quote 7.1. The concept of DMCs is useful for understanding how intensely felt motivation drives learning (Dörnyei, Muir, & Ibrahim, 2014; Dörnyei, Henry, & Muir, 2016).

Quote 7.1 Examples of DMCs in Educational Settings

In educational settings, a DMC may be found within a high-school student's intense preparation for a math competition, in a group of students' deciding to put on a drama performance at school and giving the rehearsals top priority in their lives, or in the initiation of a school campaign to support a charity or other public cause. These instances involve the establishing of a momentum towards a goal that becomes dominant in the participants' life for a period of time, and which allows both self and observers to clearly sense the presence of a powerful drive pushing action forwards.

Dornyei, Ibrahim, and Muir (2015, p. 98)

Investment

The concept of *investment* was conceptualized by Bonny Norton in the 1990s as a complement to the traditional construct of motivation as a fixed personality trait. This understanding, she argued, did not capture the complex relationship between power, identity, and language learning that she had observed in her research with five immigrant women in Canada who were taking an ESL course together (Peirce, 1995; Norton, 2000; 2011, 2013; Norton & deCosta, 2018; Norton & Toohey, 2011). From her year-long case study, which drew on data from diaries, questionnaires, interviews, and home visits, she found that while all the women wanted to learn English, their desires to use English varied depending on the social context.

Norton concluded that learners are best understood as individuals who have complex social histories and multiple desires and whose learning trajectories are therefore complex, contradictory, and ever changing. She argued that conceptions of motivation that were dominant in SLA at the time, which conceived of learners as having unified, cohesive identities, did not, and in fact could not, capture these phenomena. Drawing on a poststructuralist view of identity (Weedon, 1987), she coined the term investment to capture "the socially and historically constructed relationship of the [L2 learners] to the target language and their sometimes ambivalent desire to learn and practice it" (Peirce, 1995, p. 17).

Furthermore, drawing on Bourdieu's (1977; Bourdieu & Passeron, 1977) notion of cultural capital, Norton argued that learners who invest in learning another language may do so with the understanding that they will acquire a wider range of symbolic and material resources, which in turn will increase the value of their cultural capital and social power. By symbolic resources, Norton means language, education, and friendships; material resources refer to money, capital goods, and real estate (Norton, 2000). As the value of learners' cultural capital increases, so do their desires for the future and their investment in learning. Norton elaborates on the notion of investment in Quote 7.2.

An extension of Norton's findings on investment has to do with the *imagined communities* that L2 learners aspire to join. As discussed in Chapter 6, imagined communities refer to "groups of people, not immediately tangible and accessible, with whom we connect through the power of the imagination" (Norton, 2013, p. 8). Norton based this on data from two of the five women participants of her original study, both of whom withdrew from their ESL class during the time of Norton's original study. One woman stopped attending because she felt that she was being positioned as an immigrant, rather than as a professional, an identity she had before arriving in Canada and a community she imagined joining in Canada. The other student stopped because she felt

Quote 7.2 The Concept of Investment

The concept of investment, which I introduced in Norton Peirce (1995), signals the socially and historically constructed relationship of learners to the target language, and their often ambivalent desire to learn and practice it. It is best understood with reference to the economic metaphors that Bourdieu uses in his work—in particular, the notion of cultural capital. Bourdieu and Passeron (1977) use the term 'cultural capital' to reference to the knowledge and modes of thought that characterize different classes and groups in relation to specific sets of social forms. They argue that some forms of cultural capital have a higher exchange value than others in relation to a set of social forms which value some forms of knowledge and thought over others. If learners invest in a second language, they do so with the understanding that they will acquire a wider range of symbolic and material resources, which in turn increase the value of their cultural capital. Learners expect or hope to have a good return on that investment—a return that will give them access to hitherto unattainable resources.

Norton (2000, p. 10)

that her home country and her identity as a member of that country were marginalized in the class.

In both cases, the learners' imagined communities and identities within them conflicted with the identity positions they were ascribed in their ESL classroom, which resulted in their dropping out of the course. Norton concluded that the women's investments in learning were mediated by their imagined communities, communities that the learners believed offered them possibilities for expanding their resources, including the possibility of taking on new identities. Based on her research, Norton maintains that learners' imagined communities are as real to learners as their current communities and may even have a greater impact on their investment in L2 learning. However, she cautions, it may be that the people and communities in whom learners have the greatest investment "may be the very people who provide (or limit) access to the imagined community of a given learner" (Darvin & Norton, 2015; Norton & Toohey, 2011).

The constructs of investment and imagined communities have been fruitful to explorations of L2 learning in a range of settings (Darvin & Norton, 2015; Haneda, 2005; Kanno & Norton, 2003; Norton & Gao, 2008). For example, in her case study of two university-level learners of Japanese, Haneda (2005) found that the students were differentially invested in learning to write in Japanese. The differences, she argued, resulted from an interaction among several factors, including their learning trajectories with respect to Japanese, their attitudes toward learning Japanese, their career aspirations, and their imagined future communities.

In their study of university-level students in a Hong Kong university, Gao, Cheng, and Kelly (2008) found that through their participation in a social community named the "English Club", the students became invested in an imagined community of English speakers. This imagined community consisted not of target language English speakers, but of English-speaking Chinese who, because of their English skills, were considered elite and thus different from monolingual Chinese speakers. They concluded that investing in learning English afforded the group of students "cultural capital", that is, desired social identities for negotiating their social relationships with their peers.

As a final example, Anya (2017) studied the investments of African American language learners of Portuguese in a study abroad program that took place in the Afro-Brazilian city of Salvador. She drew on findings from her earlier study (2011), which showed that the students who were invested in learning Portuguese were drawn by the desire to connect with and learn more about Afro-descendant speakers of their target language. Findings from her study of the study abroad program showed just how the learners' investments in particular aspects of the Brazilian culture and communities gave shape to the eventual outcomes of their personal transformations during their time abroad.

Additional work has been undertaken by Norton and her colleagues to better understand student investment in digital literacy and English language learning (Early & Norton, 2014; Norton & Early, 2011; Norton & Williams, 2012; Stranger-Johannessen & Norton, 2017). The findings reveal the power of digital technologies in affording students opportunities to connect with and invest in communities that lie beyond the local and may have been unimaginable before. Norton and Williams (2012), for example, investigated the investment of secondary school students residing in a rural village in Uganda in Egranary, an offline digital library containing millions of multimedia documents that does not require connection to the internet. They found that the student participants became highly invested in the technology because it expanded the range of identities that were possible for them, both at the time of the study and in their imagined futures. As they became more proficient in using the resource, students' cultural capital and social power increased, which in turn expanded what was imaginable to them. Travel, advanced education, professional careers, and other opportunities became part of the students' imagined futures and imagined identities.

Individual Agency

Agency is the "socioculturally mediated capacity to act" (Ahearn, 2001, p. 112). "Socioculturally mediated" reflects the view that people are not agents of free will, independent decision-makers, with unfettered power and authority to use their resources to carry out any kind of action they want in any local context of action (Bucholtz & Hall, 2005; Kayi-Aydar, 2015). Rather, individual agency is a social construction, "something that has to be routinely created and sustained in the reflexive activities of the individual" (Giddens, 1991, p. 52). Social actions, then, are both structured and structuring, bound by their resources' histories of meaning and yet "creative, variable, responsive to situational exigencies and capable of producing novel consequences" (Ochs & Schieffelin, 2017, p. 8).

While all acts of meaning making involve some level of agency, the degree of individual agency we can exert in taking action is not equal across contexts. Rather, the resources we use, and agentive actions we take in shaping our identities and refashioning our relationships with others, are both afforded and constrained by specific historical, social, and contextual circumstances constituting local contexts of action. For example, in many formal learning settings, there is more authority ascribed to teachers' identities than to students' identities. Consequently, teachers have greater power and more agency to determine the types of activities and resources to which learners will be given access and the opportunities they will have to engage in the activities and use their resources. As learners' access to opportunities varies so does their L2 development. Those who are afforded more opportunities are more likely to be more positioned as "good" learners. Others who are afforded fewer opportunities are more likely to be positioned as "poor" or "resistant" learners. In such situations, learners may have little agency to reshape or resist these practices (Hall, 1997; Norton & Toohey, 2011).

The study by Dagenais, Day, and Toohey (2006) is an insightful illustration of the academic consequences of the unequal distribution of agency between teachers and students in constructing students' identities *as* students (see Chapter 6). Theirs was a longitudinal study of a learner's development of the literacy practices comprising her French and English classes in the French immersion elementary program in which the student, Sarah, was enrolled. Their findings reveal that while Sarah was active and verbal in some classroom practices, in others she was quiet and reluctant to speak and that this reluctance was differently interpreted by her teachers. One teacher evaluated Sarah's participation negatively, attributing an "at risk" identity to her. In contrast, two other teachers interpreted Sarah's reluctance to perform in large group conversations not as indications of academic difficulties. Rather, they perceived that Sarah was developing at her own pace and who "with encouragement, was poised on the edge of participation" (ibid., p. 215). These different positionings of Sarah were consequential in that the different identities were linguistically reinforced by the teachers in large group activities and small group exchanges. In both cases, Sarah had no agency to affect how she was positioned by her teachers and the academic consequences they engendered.

Many studies of L2 learners' agency have shown that learners are not always passive participants in the process of learning. Rather, they are active agents who, depending on the context, have the power to make choices, initiate certain actions, resist others, and in other ways take control over their learning in pursuit of their goals in learning an L2 (Miller, 2012, 2014; Norton, 2013; van Compernolle & McGregor, 2016). The study by Baynham (2006) of an intensive ESOL for refugees and asylum seekers in the UK illustrates this. He shows how the learners took agentive steps by disrupting their instructional interactions to raise issues they were dealing with outside of the classroom. He concludes that these "unexpected irruptions of student lived experience" (p. 37) served to create opportunities for students to talk about the ongoing challenges they were dealing with outside of the classroom and help them develop strategies to deal with them.

Such agentive acts do not always enhance learners' positions, however, as shown in Talmy's (2008) study of first-year high school ESL classes. Despite the fact that the student population in these classes included local students who were long-time residents of their community and experienced in US schooling contexts, the curriculum was structured for recently-arrived students. This mismatch between the local students' self-identifications and the ESL student identity embodied in the curriculum led to the local students' development of a range of actions that worked to subvert their official classroom activities and the identity ascribed to them by their school. These actions included refusing to complete their homework, arguing with the teacher for reduced homework loads and teasing students who did the work. Their actions over the year, however, did little to change the official school practices and to transform their identities. In fact, the students received poor grades and were labeled low-achieving, and the school continued to identify them as ESL students. Their active resistance served not to transform their identities but to reproduce them and the classroom practices they struggled against.

Summary

Motivation, investment, and agency play significant roles in mediating L2 learners' learning experiences and the development of their semiotic repertoires. Research that draws on these constructs makes clear that these are not constant or fixed properties but rather vary within and across contexts and over time. Depending on contextual circumstances, L2 learners may be differently motivated to participate in their contexts of learning. They may also be differently invested in the practices of their classrooms and the communities to which they aspire to belong. Finally, the degree of agency afforded to learners to create or take advantage of their L2 learning opportunities in specific contexts of use also changes. As learners' motivation, investment, and degree of agency vary, so do their trajectories of experiences in and outside of the classroom, and, ultimately, their academic outcomes and semiotic repertoires.

Implications for Understanding L2 Teaching

At the meso level of social activity, L2 learning is mediated by ever-changing degrees of motivation, investment, and agency. As these vary, so do learners' trajectories of learning. From this understanding of L2 learning, we can derive four implications for understanding L2 teaching.

1   Motivation plays a significant role in L2 learning. Based on his extensive research on the topic, Zoltan Dörnyei (2014) offers three principles for understanding the role that L2 teaching plays in creating a motivating learning environment. Principle One states that there is more to motivational strategies than offering rewards and punishments. Finding ways to promote learners' visions of themselves as L2 learners and users, in the long run, will be more effective than the "carrot and stick" approach. Principle Two states that once engendered, student motivation must be actively maintained and protected. Otherwise, both the teacher and learners may lose sight of their goal, leading to the gradual diminishment of motivation. Principle Three states that what counts is the quality, not the quantity, of the motivational strategies that are used. Choosing strategies that suit the teacher, the learners, and the learning environment may be sufficient to create and sustain a positive motivational climate.
2   As noted previously, a directed motivational current is an intensive determination that supports L2 learners' long-term, goal-directed L2 learning. Based on emerging findings from their developing research program on the topic, Dörnyei and his colleagues (2016; Dörnyei, Muir, & Ibrahim, 2014; Dörnyei, Ibrahim, & Muir, 2015; Henry, Davydenko, & Dörnyei, 2015), believe that L2 teaching can play a role in intentionally generating DMCs in their classrooms by facilitating intensive group projects. Project templates should include 1. a clearly defined target that is relevant and real to the students, 2. a structure that lays out a clear pathway toward the target and has a clear set of subgoals marking students' progress, and 3. supportive

cooperation among the learners that elicits positive emotionality or passion toward the project.
3   Recognizing the significant role that investment plays in L2 learning, L2 teachers must be ever mindful of how their teaching practices are linked to students' investments in their future communities and identities within them. To do this work involves regular explorations with students of their investments as L2 learners and users. What and where are their desired communities? Who are their desired future selves and how do they imagine participating in the social groups in which they have the greatest investment? Learning environments should be structured in ways that allow students to critically examine their experiences as L2 learners and users, in and outside of the classroom, and to identify opportunities and possible roadblocks to realizing their visions. More generally, L2 teaching practices should engender a learning environment that is supportive, safe, and meaningful to learners' real and imagined lives.
4   Individual agency plays a significant role in L2 learning. Recognizing the key role that learner agency plays in the process of meaning making, a multiliteracies pedagogy is aimed at creating learners who are active designers of their own meanings, and "with a sensibility open to differences, change and innovation", and, more generally, opening up "viable lifecourses for a world of change and diversity" (Cope & Kalantzis, 2009, p. 175). L2 teaching that draws on the multiliteracies framework regards all modes of representation as dynamic processes of transformation rather than processes of reproduction and learners not as reproducers of meaning but as agentive meaning makers, i.e., "fully makers and remakers of signs and transformers of meaning" (ibid.). The goal behind the purposeful choices that L2 teachers make in designing their learning contexts is to lead to the transformation of L2 learners as expert designers of their own worlds (see Chapter 8).

Pedagogical Activities

This series of pedagogical activities will assist you in relating to and making sense of the concepts that inform our understanding of *L2 learning as mediated by motivation, investment, and agency.*

Experiencing

A. Motivation and Investment

Consider how motivation and investment have played a role in your language learning experiences by discussing your responses to the following questions with a partner or in a small group.

- What motivated you to pursue the study of another language?
- What role has investment in imagined identities and communities played in your desire to learn another language?
- How have you sustained motivation to continue?
- How has your investment in your imagined identities and communities shaped your learning opportunities?
- What conclusions can you draw from your learning experiences about the role that you, as an L2 teacher, play in promoting learners' motivation and investment in L2 learning?

B. Agency

Create a visual depiction of your understanding of the construct of agency and its relationship to your learning experiences in a particular learning environment in which you are or have been a student. Then, consider the following questions:

- What contextual conditions appear to afford you more agency as a student to design your own paths of learning?
- Which appear to constrain your agency?
- What conclusions can you draw from your own experiences about the role that you as a teacher can play in promoting L2 learners' agency as "meaning- maker[s]-as-designer[s]" (Cope & Kalantzis, 2009, p. 177).

Conceptualizing

A. Concept Development

Select two of the concepts listed in Box 7.1. Craft a definition of each of the two concepts in your own words. Create one or two concrete examples of each concept that you have either experienced first-hand or can imagine. Pose one or two questions that you still have about the concepts and develop a way to gather more information.

Box 7.1 Concepts: L2 learning is mediated by motivation, investment, and agency

agency	motivation
directed motivational current	investment
L2 motivational self system	

B. Concept Development

Choose one of the concepts from the previous activity on which to gather additional information. Using the internet, search for information about the concept. Create a list of five or so facts about it. These can include names of scholars who study the concept, studies that have been done on the concept along with their findings, visual images depicting the concept, and so on. Create a concept web that visually records the information you gathered from your explorations.

Analyzing

A. Directed Motivational Current

Locate two studies published in the last five years on the concept of directed motivational current. Summarize each study, using the table in Figure 7.1 to organize the information. Based on your readings of the studies, consider the following questions:

- What kind of connections can you make between directed motivational currents and the concepts of investment and agency?
- How useful is the construct for understanding L2 learning? What are its limitations?
- What implications can you draw for L2 teaching?

B. Motivation, Investment, and Agency

Imagine you are the teacher of a high school or adult-level ESL classroom with 20 or so multilingual students who have varied educational backgrounds and come from various parts of the world. You have a few individuals who appear to be resistant to participating. They remain quiet in small group discussions, and they reluctantly respond when called upon. You know how important participation is to their academic success. How do you help them build the

Author	Research questions/focus	Terms and definitions	Participants, sources of data	Findings	Conclusions	Implications

Figure 7.1 Research study summary table.

academic competence for participating in class that they need to succeed in your course? Design two or three strategies for working with the students that take into account at least one of the following constructs: motivation, investment, and agency.

Applying

A. Investment

In small groups, create a 5–7-minute audio file directed to L2 learners on the topic of investment and how investment in imagined identities and communities shapes learning. You can decide on the format of the audio file, e.g., interview, multi-host show, roundtable discussion, etc. You can also decide on whether you want to gear your show to a specific group of learners or if your show will speak to a wide audience of learners. For ideas on developing your file, search the internet, using *podcast* and *audio files* as search terms. Once completed, share your file with your classmates. As a class, create a plan for disseminating your files to potential users.

B. Investment

Design a 2–3-minute multimodal digital story about your imagined professional identity as a language teacher and your imagined school community. Digital stories are brief personal narratives told through words, videos, images, music, and sounds and using digital technology. Before beginning, gather "how-to" information and tap into available digital resources by searching the internet. In your story, draw on the concepts presented in this chapter and in previous chapters to describe and explain your goals and visions. Once completed, share with your classmates and together design a means to showcase and publish your stories for a wider audience.

References

Ahearn, L. (2001). Language and agency. *Annual Review of Anthropology, 30*, 109–137.

Anya, U. (2011). Connecting with communities of learners and speakers: Integrative ideals, experiences, and motivations of successful Black second language learners. *Foreign Language Annals, 44*(3), 441–466.

Anya, U. (2017). *Racialized identities in second language learning: Speaking blackness in Brazil.* Oxford: Taylor & Francis.

Baynham, M. (2006). Agency and contingency in the language learning of refugees and asylum seekers. *Linguistics and Education, 17*(1), 24–39.

Bourdieu, P. (1977). The economics of linguistic exchanges. *Social Science Information, 16*(6), 645–668.

Bourdieu, P., & Passeron, J. (1977). *Reproduction in education, society, and culture.* London/Beverly Hills, CA: Sage Publications.

Bucholtz, M., & Hall, K. (2005). Identity and interaction: A sociocultural linguistic approach. *Discourse Studies, 7*(4–5), 585–614.

Cope, B., & Kalantzis, M. (2009). "Multiliteracies": New literacies, new learning. *Pedagogies: An International Journal, 4*(3), 164–195.

Dagenais, D., Day, E., & Toohey, K. (2006). A multilingual child's literacy practices and contrasting identities in the figured worlds of French immersion classrooms. *International Journal of Bilingual Education and Bilingualism, 9*(2), 205–218.

Darvin, R., & Norton, B. (2015). Identity and a model of investment in applied linguistics. *Annual Review of Applied Linguistics, 35,* 36–56.

Dobs, A. (2016). *A conversation analytic approach to motivation: Fostering motivation in the L2 classroom through play.* Unpublished doctoral thesis/dissertation

Dörnyei, Z. (2009). The L2 motivational self system. In Z. Dörnyei & E. Ushioda (Eds.), *Motivation, language identity and the L2 self* (pp. 9–42). Bristol: Multilingual Matters.

Dörnyei, Z. (2014). Motivation in second language learning. In M. Celce-Murcia, D. M. Brinton & M. A. Snow (Eds.), *Teaching English as a second or foreign language* (4th ed., pp. 518–531). Boston, MA: National Geographic Learning/Cengage Learning.

Dörnyei, Z., Henry, A., & Muir, C. (2016). *Motivational currents in language learning: Frameworks for focused interventions.* New York: Routledge/Taylor & Francis.

Dörnyei, Z., Ibrahim, Z., & Muir, C. (2015). Directed motivational currents: Regulating complex dynamic systems through motivational surges. In Z. Dörnyei, P. D. MacIntyre & A. Henry (Eds.), *Motivational dynamics in language learning* (pp. 95–105). Bristol: Multilingual Matters.

Dörnyei, Z., & Kubanyiova, M. (2014). *Motivating learners, motivating teachers: Building vision in the language classroom.* Cambridge: Cambridge University Press.

Dörnyei, Z., Muir, C., & Ibrahim, Z. (2014). Directed motivational currents: Energising language learning by creating intense motivational pathways. In D. Lasagabaster, A. Doiz, & J. M. Sierra (Eds.), *Motivation and foreign language learning: From theory to practice* (pp. 9–29). Amsterdam: John Benjamins Publishing Company.

Early, M., & Norton, B. (2014). Revisiting English as medium of instruction in rural African classrooms. *Journal of Multilingual and Multicultural Development, 35*(7), 674–691.

Gao, X., Cheng, H., & Kelly, P. (2008). Supplementing an uncertain investment?: Mainland Chinese students practising English together in Hong Kong. *Journal of Asian Pacific Communication, 18*(1), 9–29.

Giddens, A. (1991). *Modernity and self-identity: Self and society in the late modern age.* Stanford, CA: Stanford University Press.

Hall, J. K. (1997). Differential teacher attention to student utterances: The construction of different opportunities for learning in the IRF, *Linguistics & Education, 9,* 287–311.

Haneda, M. (2005). Investing in foreign-language writing: A study of two multicultural learners. *Journal of Language, Identity, and Education*, 4(4), 269–290.
Henry, A., Davydenko, S., & Dörnyei, Z. (2015). The anatomy of directed motivational currents: Exploring intense and enduring periods of L2 motivation. *The Modern Language Journal*, 99, 329–345.
Kanno, Y., & Norton, B. (Eds.) (2003). *Journal of Language, Identity, and Education*. Special issue on imagined communities and educational possibilities. 2(4).
Kayi-Aydar, H. (2015). "He's the star!": Positioning as a tool of analysis to investigate agency and access to learning opportunities in a classroom environment. In P. Deters, X. Gao, E. Miller & G. Vitanova (Eds.), *Theorizing and analyzing agency in second language learning: Interdisciplinary approaches* (pp. 133–153). Clevedon: Multilingual Matters.
Lee, N., Mikesell, L., Joaquin, A. D. L., Mates, A. W., & Schumann, J. H. (2009). *The interactional instinct: The evolution and acquisition of language*. Oxford: Oxford University Press.
Miller, E. R. (2012). Agency, language learning and multilingual spaces. *Multilingua*, 31(4), 441–468.
Miller, E. R. (2014). *The language of adult immigrants: Agency in the making*. Bristol: Multilingual Matters.
Muir, C., & Dörnyei, Z. (2013). Directed Motivational Currents: Using vision to create effective motivational pathways. *Studies in Second Language Learning and Teaching*, 3, 357–375.
Peirce, B.N. (1995). Social identity, investment and language learning. *TESOL Quarterly*, 29, 9–31.
Norton, B. (2000). *Identity and language learning*. Harlow: Pearson Education.
Norton, B. (2013). Identity and second language acquisition. In C. Chapelle (Ed.), *Encyclopedia of Applied Linguistics*. New York: Wiley-Blackwell.
Norton, B., & De Costa, P. I. (2018). Research tasks on identity in language learning and teaching. *Language Teaching*, 51(1), 90–112.
Norton, B., & Early, M. (2011). Researcher identity, narrative inquiry, and language teaching research. *TESOL Quarterly*, 45, 415–439.
Norton, B., & Gao, Y. (2008). Identity, investment, and Chinese learners of English. *Journal of Asian Pacific Communication*, 18(1), 109–120.
Norton, B., & Toohey, K. (2011). Identity, language learning, and social change. *Language Teaching*, 44, 412–446.
Norton, B., & Williams, C. J. (2012). Digital identities, student investments and eGranary as a placed resource. *Language and Education*, 26(4), 315–329.
Ochs, E., & Schieffelin, B. (2017). Language socialization: An historical overview. In P. Duff & S. May (Eds.), *Language socialization*, 3rd edition (pp. 3–16). Cham: Springer.
Richards, K. (2006). "Being the teacher": Identity and classroom conversation. *Applied Linguistics*, 27(1), 51–77.
Ryan, S., & Dörnyei, Z. (2013). The long-term evolution of language motivation and the L2 self. *Fremdsprachen in der Perspektive lebenslangen Lernens* (pp. 89–100). Frankfurt: Peter Lang.
Schumann, J. H. (2010). Applied linguistics and the neurobiology of language. In R. Kaplan (Ed.), *The Oxford handbook of applied linguistics* (pp. 244–260). Oxford: Oxford University Press.

Stranger-Johannessen, E., & Norton, B. (2017). The African storybook and language teacher identity in digital times. *The Modern Language Journal*, *101*(S1), 45–60.

Talmy, S. (2008). The cultural productions of the ESL student at Tradewinds High: Contingency, multidirectionality, and identity in L2 socialization. *Applied Linguistics*, *29*(4), 619–644.

Usioda, E., & Dörnyei, Z. (2009). Motivation, language identities and the L2 self: A Theoretical overview. In Z. Dörnyei & E. Ushioda (Eds.), *Motivation, language identity and the L2 self* (pp. 1–8). Bristol: Multilingual Matters.

Van Compernolle, R. A., & McGregor, J. (Eds.) (2016). *Authenticity, language and interaction in second language contexts*. New York: Multilingual Matters.

Weedon, C. (1987). *Feminist practice and poststructuralist theory*. New York: Basil Blackwell.

Chapter 8

L2 Learning Is Mediated by Literacy and Instructional Practices

Overview

In Chapter 5, we discussed how individual repertoires are shaped by the various processes involved in primary language socialization. While L2 socialization shares the same principles as L1 socialization, the process is more complicated. This is due to the fact that adolescents and adults who are learning another language come to their L2 learning experiences already in possession of diverse repertoires of semiotic resources, cultural traditions, and community affiliations (Duff, 2007). It is also complicated by the fact that for many learners, their L2 learning experiences take place outside of the family, largely in educational institutions where instructional and literacy practices are prime sources of influence on L2 learning. In this chapter we examine the roles that these factors play in mediating both the processes and outcomes of L2 learning.

Literacy

Traditionally, SLA studies of L2 literacy were concerned primarily with the cognitive processes entailed in learning to read and write in another language (Grabe & Stoller, 2011; Young-Scholten, 2013). From the abundance of SLA research on the cognitive complexities of learning to become literate in another language, we know that developing literacy skills in another language depends on general and domain specific cognitive mechanisms such as selective attention, working memory, metalinguistic awareness, and comprehension monitoring. We also know that the development of literate skills and oral skills are interdependent and that the process of becoming biliterate is more cognitively complicated when learning to read and write in languages with different writing systems (Koda, 2005; Tarone, Bigelow, & Hansen, 2009; Tarone & Bigelow, 2005).

During the latter part of the twentieth century a more expanded understanding of literacy emerged in SLA, an understanding that was informed by research from such fields as anthropology, education, linguistics, and cultural psychology exploring relationships between cognition and oral and written social practices (e.g., Barton & Hamilton, 1998; Cook-Gumperz, 1986; Scollon & Scollon, 1981). Contemporary understandings view literacy not just as a cognitive phenomenon, something that happens inside one's head, but as a social phenomenon as well, as ways of participating in social groups (Gee, 2010). Nor is literacy one set of technical skills for reading and writing; instead it is a set of social practices, of *literacies*, that are situated within and patterned by their social, institutional, and cultural contexts. Moreover, written texts do not stand alone. Gee (2010) notes that within different practices, written texts are "integrated with different ways of using oral language; different ways of acting and interacting; different ways of knowing, valuing, and believing; and often different ways of using various tools and technologies" (p. 166). Literacies and the ways of reading and writing they make possible are not universal but are multiple and varied, designed for different purposes by social groups and so are "different facets of doing life" (Lankshear & Knobel, 2011, p. 13).

Individuals develop skills for participating in their literacy practices just as they learn language: by being socialized into the literacy practices of their social and cultural groups. In their participation, they develop a range of semiotic resources for producing and understanding the many ways of representing knowledge (Jewitt & Kress, 2003; Gee, 2010; Halliday, 1978). At the same time, they develop understandings of the affordances and constraints of the resources, and, more generally, of the values placed on the practices by their social groups. They learn how to act, know, believe, and value in "ways that 'go with' how they write and read" (Gee, 2010, p. 167).

This understanding of literacy has informed a substantial body of work comparing the home literacies of learners to the literacies of schools. One of the earliest and most influential studies is the study by Shirley Brice Heath (1983). Heath's study was a longitudinal investigation comparing the language and literacy expectations, values, and practices of two rural, working-class communities with those found in their schools. She found that in the rural communities, children were socialized into ways of using language and texts that differed fairly significantly from those in schools. School practices more closely mirrored the language and literacy practices of the urban, middle-class communities in which the schools were located. These differences, she argued, resulted in different learning outcomes in school. Children from the rural communities had more difficulty succeeding academically than did their urban counterparts, whose home language and literacy practices more closely resembled those of school. This was so, Heath argued, because the contexts of schooling were a natural extension of the home contexts of the middle-class children. Consequently, the children were able to use what they had learned at home as a foundation for their learning in schools, whereas those from the rural communities could not.

This work has continued to inform research exploring learners' home and school literacy practices (e.g., Phillips, 1983; McCarty & Watahomigie, 1998; Martin-Jones & Bhatt, 1998; Barton, Hamilton, & Ivanic, 2000; Maybin, 2008; Moll et al., 1992; Ortlieb & Cheek, 2017). Together, the findings are clear: learners whose home and school literacy practices differ do not perform as well as those learners whose practices are more similar. The reason for the differences in performances is not because some home practices are inherently inferior; rather, it is more a matter of compatibility. Learners whose home language and literacy activities reflect the dominant practices of schools are likely to have more opportunities for success since they only need to build on and extend what they have learned at home (Hall, 2008).

On the other hand, learners who are socialized into language and literacy practices that differ from schooling practices are likely to have more difficulty since they will need to add additional repertoires of practices to those they already know. In these cases, institutional perspective also plays a role. In institutions where learners' home language and literacy practices are perceived as resources to be drawn on, difficulties are often diminished. In contrast, in institutions where learners' practices are perceived as obstacles to be overcome, difficulties are often intensified (Barton & Hamilton, 1998).

Recognizing the value of learners' home language and literacies for school-based learning, a growing body of research has explored ways of linking learners' out-of-school multilingual language and literacy practices more closely to mainstream school practices (Gutiérrez, Baquedano-López, & Tejeda, 1999; Moll et al., 1992; Moje et al., 2004; Kenner & Ruby, 2012; Pahl, 2014). An early example of this is the work of Luis Moll and his colleagues (1992; Moll, Amanti, Neff, & Gonzalez, 2005). He argued that the home and community practices of students were rich resources of sophisticated language and literacy practices that should be drawn on rather than ignored in the academic practices of schools. He called for research into learners' *funds of knowledge* and for the development of innovations that use the funds to transform school curricula.

Linking minority learners' home and community experiences and their rich multilingual repertoires to those of schools has been proven to increase learners' motivation and academic success. The study by Kenner and Ruby (2012) illustrates this. They brought together four teachers from complementary schools in the UK with two teachers from mainstream schools to plan lessons that became part of the curriculum in both schools. Complementary schools are supplementary or Saturday language schools in the UK. They offer language instruction to immigrant and ethnic minority learners to help them maintain their home languages. In the United States, they are usually referred to as heritage-language or community-based schools. Through the teachers' collaborative efforts, they designed a multilingual syncretic curriculum, which included the following topics: poems and stories with parallel themes in different languages; learning about plants through gardening; fruits and vegetables found in different countries; and jobs in different countries. The study demonstrated the key role that the partnership between the mainstream and complementary teachers played in enhancing the children's opportunities to draw on the full range of their capacities for learning, thereby challenging the "institutional constraints of a monolingualizing education system" (ibid., p. 414).

Digital Literacies

Fueled by the proliferation of digital technologies such as computers, video games, smart phones, and the internet, the shapes and purposes of literacy practices have expanded well beyond conventional print literacies. The ways in which individuals interpret and make meaning via these digital technologies are increasingly multimodal, with graphic, pictorial, audio, physical, and spatial patterns of meaning integrated within or even supplanting traditional written texts (Gee, 2010; Lankshear & Knobel, 2011).

Digital tools have not only transformed the means for producing, distributing, and interpreting meaning via orthographic scripts; they have changed the very nature of what counts as a text. These tools enable individuals to make and interpret meanings in ways that go beyond face-to-face settings and "'travel' across space and time" (Lankshear & Knobel, 2011, p. 40). Devices such as mobile phones, smart pads and computers, multiplayer online games, and virtual social networking sites such as Facebook and Second Life have not only given individuals access to people and communities, and to information from around the world. They have also given rise to new types of literacies, including texting, tweeting, Facebooking, video gaming, producing websites and podcasting, to name just a few (Gee, 2012; Kern, 2015; Thorne, Fischer, & Lu, 2012). The term *digital literacies* captures these new literacies. It is defined as "the practices of communicating, relating, thinking and 'being' associated with digital media" (Jones & Hafner, 2012, p. 13).

Exploring L2 learners' digital multilingual, multimodal literacies has become an increasingly important focus of L2 socialization research (Reinhardt & Thorne, 2017). Findings from these studies show how in various digital contexts such as online fanfiction communities, Facebook communities, and online game communities, individuals construct new multilingual and multimodal literacy practices that transcend boundaries and through these practices, create new identities and new relationships (e.g., Chik, 2014; Jonsson & Muhonen, 2014; Lam, 2009; Reinhardt & Thorne, 2017; Steinkuehler, 2008; Thorne, 2008). The term *transnational literacies* has been coined to refer to the practices that extend across national borders (Hornberger & Link, 2012; Warriner, 2007).

The abundance of digital innovations and the speed at which they continue to be developed have made even more complex the connections between home and school literacy practices. Also adding to the complexity are the changing demographics of communities. Contemporary communities are more linguistically and culturally diverse, comprising families of diverse unions, with members who are bilingual and multilingual and who have ties to multiple cultural groups. Findings from studies examining these communities reveal that their home practices are equally diverse, distinguished by the use of *translingual practices*, that is, two or more languages and a range of digital tools in addition to print in the creation, distribution, and use of complex transnational texts (Canagarajah, 2013; and see, for example, the studies by Barlett, 2007; McGinnis et al., 2007; Harris, 2003; Lam, 2004, 2009; Moore, 1999; Zentella, 1997).

L2 Socialization in Educational Settings

Scholars interested in L2 learning in schools have used the theoretical framework and methods of language socialization, detailed in Chapter 5, and the comparative studies of home and school practices as a springboard for research on the language and literacy practices found in L2 classrooms and their consequences for learner development (Duff, 1995, 1996, 2002; Harklau, 1994, 2002; Huang, 2004; Kanagy, 1999; Moore, 1999; Morita, 2000; Ohta, 1999; Poole, 1992; Smythe & Toohey, 2009). This research draws attention to the important role that the language and literacy practices of educational settings play in shaping not only L2 learners' academic success but, as importantly, their understandings of the academic world and their places within it, their status relative to teachers and peers, and the relative legitimacy of their cultural and linguistic resources (Toohey, Day, & Manyak, 2007; Harklau, 2007).

An early study examining the relationship between classroom practices and L2 learning is Harklau's (1994) comparative study of the language and literacy practices found in ESL and mainstream classrooms. She found significant differences in terms of the curricula content and goals and instructional practices. She argued that these differences had different socializing effects leading to the marginalization of the ESL learners. Willett (1995) and Toohey (1998) reported similar findings.

They examined the socialization practices of mainstream elementary classrooms that included ESL learners and found that the teachers' varying perceptions of the learners' language and literacy abilities led to differentiation in the kinds of learning opportunities that the teachers made available to the students. This variation, in turn, led to differences in the children's academic development.

Additional studies have shown that the processes and outcomes of socializing processes in educational settings are not stable, static, or unidirectional. Nor are learners passive recipients. Rather, L2 socialization is dynamic and multidirectional; where L2 learners' motivations and resources diverge from those of the experts, the processes can be conflictual, and outcomes can vary, ranging from high levels of acculturation to variable levels marked by resistance or ambivalence (Duff, 2012; Miller & Zuengler, 2011). Studies by Hall (2004) and Canagarajah (2004), for example, reveal how students responded to what they perceived to be marginalizing forces of the official classroom practices by creating "safe houses" (Canagarajah, 2004, p. 12) in the classroom, speaking softly to neighbouring seatmates, catching up on work for other classes, and in other ways living quietly on the margins of the classroom (also refer to Talmy's 2008 study, which was summarized in Chapter 7).

The increasing numbers of L2 learners attending secondary and post-secondary schools over the last two decades or so have presented new opportunities for research on L2 socialization in educational settings. Since the turn into the twenty-first century, research on the socialization processes and outcomes for these groups of students in various discipline-related academic events such as oral presentations, small group work, and thesis and dissertation writing activities has burgeoned (e.g., Duff & Kobayashi, 2010; Kobayashi, 2006, 2016; Seloni, 2011, 2014; Vickers, 2007; Yang, 2010; Zappa-Hollman, 2007; Zappa-Hollman & Duff, 2014).

Yang (2010), for example, examined the various practices by which L2 university-level undergraduate students were socialized into competent performance in their academic oral presentations. Seloni (2014) followed the academic socialization practices one mature multilingual writer engaged in as he completed his M.A. thesis. Zappa-Hollman and Duff (2014) examined the socialization of three L2 students into the academic culture of a Canadian university and found that students' relationships with peers were key factors in their successful socialization. Together, the findings from this body of research reveal the linguistic, social, and cultural challenges these L2 learners face in their contexts of learning and the high stakes associated with their performances in their disciplinary academic discourses and their academic success. They also show the role that variation in learners' access to opportunities within a classroom or across classrooms plays in mediating learners' investment in these contexts (Darvin & Norton, 2015; Morita, 2004). The findings notwithstanding, recognizing the ever-changing demographics of communities world-wide, scholars in this field have called for continued research on academic language and literacy socialization and, in particular, in non-Western communities (Duff & Anderson, 2015; Moore, 2017).

In sum, studies of educational settings that draw on the language socialization paradigm add to understandings of how learners develop the semiotic resources and values of L2 language and literacy practices through their recurring engagement in social activities with other social group members, including peers and more experienced members. The processes are not uniform or stable, but are dynamic and multidirectional, and can lead learners to "new ways of acting, being, and thinking that do not simply reproduce the repertoire of cultural, linguistic, and ideological practices to which they are exposed" (Lee & Bucholtz, 2015, p. 323).

Mediational Role of Classroom Interaction

Interaction between teachers and students in L2 classrooms is one of the primary means by which socialization is accomplished. A great deal of research has focused specifically on the interactional routines of teacher-student interactions. Findings from a wide range of classrooms has revealed that a common instructional routine that mediates student learning opportunities is the specialized teacher-led three-action sequence labeled the IRF (e.g., Duff, 1995; Hall, 1995, 1998, 2004; Haneda, 2004; Lin, 1999a, 1999b; Mehan & Griffin, 1980; Mondada & Pekarek, 2004; Waring, 2008, 2009). The exchange involves the teacher eliciting information (I) from students in order to ascertain whether and how well they know the material. The teacher does this by asking a question or issuing a directive to which students are expected to provide a response (R). The third action provides some form of feedback (F) on student responses by, for example, using positive assessment terms such as *good* and *right*, prompting self-correction by the student and so on (Haneda, 2005; Lee, 2007; Nassaji & Wells, 2000; Wells, 1993). The third turns can also do additional work by, for example, asking students to clarify, elaborate, or defend their responses.

Research has shown that when the third turn is restricted to assessing the student's response, learning opportunities are limited (Hall, 1995, 2004; Waring, 2008; 2009). For example, in her study of a high school foreign language classroom, Hall (1995) found that learning opportunities in the IRF were pervasively limited to short responses to simple teacher questions that did little more than ask students to list familiar objects or respond to simple yes-or-no questions. Student responses rarely extended beyond short phrases or clauses and, in giving their responses, students rarely had to attend to other students' contributions. An example of this type of teacher-student interaction is illustrated in Figure 8.1. As shown here, the teacher asks students the same simple question, *do you like to sing*, which elicits a simple response by the students. In turn, the response elicits a positive evaluation by the teacher in the form of a repetition of the student's response. Hall concluded that extensive use of this pattern of interaction afforded students very limited opportunities to develop anything other than very linguistically and cognitively simple resources for making meaning in Spanish.

In contrast to the limited opportunities for student participation afforded by the type of interaction illustrated in Figure 8.1, findings show that where the third turn follows up on student responses by

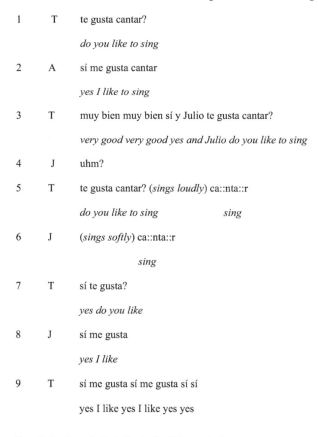

Figure 8.1 Restricted third turns.
Source: Hall (1995, p. 44).

321	T:	They ((some students)) say no, the plant will NOT grow because it needs water and light. OK I did give it some water. It has water but it does not have light. Um, ((calling out a group's name)) what do YOU say?
322	April:	Um I think um it will grow for a little while then it – then it – then it will
323	T:	Ok, I like the way April said that but some people were not listening. Can you say that again?
324	April:	I think i – it will grow for a little while but maybe for a couple of weeks it will die.
325	T:	She thinks it will grow for a while but then it will die. Why?
326	April:	Because it wouldn't get no light.
327	T:	Ok, an idea, anyone else have an idea about what's going to happen?

Key: T = teacher; April = student

Figure 8.2 Teacher uptake of student responses.
Source: Haneda (2005, pp. 324–325).

asking them to do additional work such as elaborate, clarify, and make connections, opportunities for learning are enhanced (e.g., Boyd & Maloof, 2000; Boxer & Cortes-Conde, 2000; Haneda, 2005; Lee, 2007). For example, in her study of the teacher-student interactions in an ESL science lesson in an elementary school, Haneda showed how teacher uptake of student responses in the third turn provided students with more opportunities to contribute to the lesson. Figure 8.2 is an excerpt from Haneda's study that illustrates teacher uptake of student responses.

According to Haneda, the excerpt illustrates several actions performed by teacher turns following the teacher question in turn 321. First, she asks April to repeat her response, apparently so that others can hear her (turn 323). She then asks April to explain her reasoning for her prediction (turn 325), and after April's response, she invites others to contribute other alternatives (turn 327). Then the teacher wraps up the sequence by summarizing the preceding discussion (turn 327). Haneda concluded that such actions afforded more opportunities to students to contribute and to provide answers that are more sophisticated, and thus facilitated students' learning of both content and language.

Scaffolding

Scaffolding is a term that has been used to refer to the mediating role of classroom interaction. It was originally coined by Wood, Bruner, and Ross (1976) to refer to the process by which experts assist novices to achieve a goal or solve a problem that the novices could not achieve or solve alone. The process comprises six functions, which are used by experts in their interactions with novices to negotiate the parameters of a task, assess novices' levels of competence relative to the task and determine the types of assistance they need to complete the task. The six functions are (Wood et al., p. 98):

1. Recruitment: Enlisting the novice's interest in and attention to the task.
2. Reduction in degrees of freedom: Simplifying the task by reducing the number of acts needed to complete it.
3. Direction maintenance: Maintaining the novice's motivation and progress toward the goals of the task.
4. Marking critical features: Calling the novice's attention to relevant aspects of the task.
5. Frustration control: Decreasing the novice's stress.
6. Demonstration: Demonstrating or modeling solutions to the task.

The goal of scaffolding is to eventually hand the responsibility for task completion to the learner. The term has been tied to the concept of zone of proximal development (ZPD), a key term of Vygotsky's theory of development. Vygotsky argued that determining what a child can do on her own gives an incomplete picture of cognitive development as it only reveals what the child can do. Also essential is determining what the child can do with assistance from others as this provides insight into the child's abilities that are in the process of forming (Minick, 1987; Lantolf & Poehner, 2004; Vygotsky, 1998). These tasks are accomplishing by finding children's zones of proximal development. Vygotsky (1978, p. 86) defined the ZPD as

> the distance between the actual developmental level as determined by independent problem solving and the level of potential development as determined through problem-solving under adult guidance, or in collaboration with more capable peers.

McCormick and Donato (2000) drew on Wood et al.'s (1976) notion of scaffolding in their study of teacher questions in a university-level ESL classroom. They found that teacher questions served several purposes, such as marking critical features and reducing the degrees of freedom when there was a breakdown in communication between the teacher and students. Other questions were used to maintain students' motivation and keep discussions going. Additional studies have found that scaffolding in the L2 classroom is not limited to teacher-student interactions but can also occur in peer interactions, with learners scaffolding each other's learning to jointly solve problems and complete tasks (e.g., Antón & DiCamilla, 1998; Davin & Donato, 2013; De Guerrero & Villamil, 2000; DiCamilla & Antón, 1997).

Mediation

Some have critiqued the metaphor of scaffolding as being limited in its ability to capture the full picture of the ZPD in that it leads to a view of adult-child interactions as too one-sided with the adult constructing the scaffold alone and presenting it for the use of the novice (Stone, 1998). A related criticism is that it does not emphasize the ways in which the dynamics of scaffolding change as a function of the novice's involvement (ibid). In fact, as pointed out by Stone (1998), Vygotsky never used the scaffolding metaphor.

James Lantolf, a renowned scholar of Vygotsky's theory of development in the field of SLA, with his colleagues use the term *mediation*, a core concept of Vygotsky's theory (1978, 1981), to refer to the contingent and graduated support that is provided by teachers and other experts (see Chapter 5). According to Vygotsky's theory, all human psychological processes are mediated by tools such as language, and other semiotic resources. In the course of their activities together, children are socialized into adopting and using the tools, which then function as mediators of the children's more advanced psychological processes (Karpov & Haywood, 1998; Lantolf & Thorne, 2006).

One of the earliest studies in SLA to examine the role of mediation in L2 development from a Vygotskian perspective is that by Aljaafreh and Lantolf (1994). They report on the L2 development of three university-level ESL students as they received corrective feedback in interactions with a tutor over six tutorial sessions. The goal of the sessions was to promote learner development through provision of such mediational means as hints, cues, prompts, corrections, and explanations on formulating specific L2 grammatical features in the students' written essays. Such graduated mediation, according to Aljaafreh and Lantolf, allows the tutor and learner to discover and work within the learner's ZPD.

Analysis of the interactions between the tutor and each of the students revealed 12 levels of help provided by the tutor that ranged from very implicit, e.g., prompting the learner to read the sentence containing an error, to very explicit, e.g., providing corrections and explanations. They concluded that while all types of feedback are potentially appropriate for learning, "types of error correction (i.e., implicit or explicit) that promote learning cannot be determined independently of individual learners interacting with other individuals" (ibid., p. 480).

These findings on the mediational role of corrective feedback were reinforced by Lantolf, Kurzt, and Kisselev (2016), who reanalyzed the original data from Aljaafreh's (1992) dissertation on which Aljaafreh and Lantolf (1994) is based. They concluded that development in a second language is demonstrated in more than just linguistic performance. Also relevant are shifts in the quantity and quality of mediation provided by the expert interlocutor and the nature of learner contributions in response to the mediational process.

Instructional Approaches

There is a long history of research in SLA examining the efficacy of various instructional approaches. Findings show that while communicative approaches may provide motivation and offer plenty of opportunity for language use, they are inadequate in promoting L2 learning. This is because they do not intentionally call learners' attention to L2 constructions that learners may not perceive on their own. Recall, in Chapter 2, it was noted that L2 constructions that are not salient in the L2 environment or essential for understanding will be learned very slowly, if at all (Schmidt, 1990; Ellis, 2002, 2008). What learners need are maximum opportunities not only to use the L2 but, as importantly, to focus their attention on constructions that would otherwise go unnoticed and unlearned.

For a number of years, L2 educators have advocated task-based approaches to L2 instruction as the ideal way to bring learners' attention to particular constructions within meaningful, purposeful communication (Breen & Candlin, 1980; Doughty & Pica, 1986; Ellis, 2003, 2009; Gass, Mackey, & Ross-Feldman, 2005; Long & Crookes, 1993; Mackey & Gass, 2006; Prabhu, 1987; Skehan, 1996). In fact, there is abundant research showing instructional practices that combine explicit instruction that draw learners' attention to L2 constructions that they may not notice or may be blocked by cues in their first language with meaning-making activities are powerful learning environments (Grabe & Zhang, 2016; Schleppegrell, 2013; and see Bowles & Adams, 2015; Kim, 2015, and Robinson, 2011 for reviews of literature on task-based learning).

One approach that has garnered a great deal of attention from both researchers and teachers for bringing together meaningful tasks and explicit instruction is the Task-Based Language Teaching (TBLT) approach. What distinguishes TBLT from other task-based approaches to L2 learning is that curricular goals, instructional activities, and assessments are organized around real-world target tasks designated by particular groups of L2 learners as those that they need to or want to be able to do in the L2. Michael Long (2014), one of the first scholars in SLA to bring attention to the importance of real world tasks in the design of instructional approaches, explains what tasks are in TBLT in Quote 8.1. These are different from *task-supported* approaches, in which activities labeled as tasks are typically unconnected to students' real-world activities outside the classroom.

> **Quote 8.1 What Are Tasks in TBLT?**
>
> TBLT starts with a task-based needs analysis to identify the *target tasks* for a particular group of learners – what they need to be able to *do* in the new language. In other words, 'task' in TBLT has its normal, non-technical meaning. Tasks are the real-world activities people think of when planning, conducting, or recalling their day. That can mean things like brushing their teeth, preparing breakfast, reading a newspaper, taking a child to school, responding to e-mail messages, making a sales call, attending a lecture or a business meeting, having lunch with a colleague from work, helping a child with homework, coaching a soccer team, and watching a TV program. Some tasks are mundane, some complex. Some require language use, some do not; for others, it is optional.
> Long (2014, p. 6, emphasis in the original)

Rod Ellis (2009, p. 242), a prominent scholar of language teaching research in the field of SLA, offers what he considers to be advantages that the TBLT approach has over other language teaching approaches:

1. It offers the opportunity for "natural" learning inside the classroom.
2. It emphasizes meaning over form but can also cater for learning form.
3. It affords learners a rich input of target language.
4. It is intrinsically motivating.
5. It is compatible with a learner-centered educational philosophy but also allows for teacher input and direction.
6. It caters to the development of communicative fluency while not neglecting accuracy.
7. It can be used alongside a more traditional approach.

There is clear evidence that how tasks are designed and how they are implemented in classrooms mediate how learners interact during the tasks and that these factors mediate the development of their L2 repertoires. What still needs to be determined is how well TBLT works in diverse instructional settings and with learners from diverse backgrounds and with diverse goals for L2 learning (Kim, 2015).

A broader instructional approach is the *pedagogy of multiliteracies* (New London Group, 1996; Cope & Kalantzis, 2009, 2015). First proposed in 1996 by a group of international scholars called the New London Group, this approach has been elaborated on by two of the co-authors of that paper, Bill Cope and Mary Kalantzis. The approach is based on the premise that the goal of teaching and learning is the transformation of learners into active designers of their own meanings. It is organized around the concept of *designing*, defined as the interested, motivated, and purposive act of meaning making. Design is forward-looking, "a means of projecting an individual's interest into their world with the intent of effect in the future" (Kress, 2010, p. 23).

In a multiliteracies pedagogy, instruction integrates all semiotic modes of representation and is organized around four knowledge processes that move from the known to the unknown and facilitate concept building and critical analysis, reflection and application of knowledge and understandings (see Chapter 1 for an explanation of how we used the framework to organize the pedagogical activities of each chapter of this text). Unlike traditional pedagogical approaches, the multiliteracies approach considers critical analysis and reflection to be essential to learners' development of critical stances toward their resources and their development as agents of social change and transformation.

The multiliteracies approach has been the topic of a small but growing body of research in SLA (e.g., Ajayi, 2008; Allen & Paesani, 2010; Hepple et al., 2014; Lotherington & Jenson, 2011; Zapata & Lacorte, 2017). For example, Lotherington (2012) documents the efforts of a group of elementary school teachers in Canada with whom she collaborated on an action research project to refashion their classroom literacy practices using the multiliteracies pedagogy. The study by Hepple et al. (2014) documents how teachers used the multiliteracies approach with a group of adolescent English language learners as a way to meet the students' diverse language and literacy needs. Zapata and Lecorte's (2017) book is a collection of empirical studies on the application of the multiliteracies approach to the teaching of Spanish to heritage speakers in the United States.

Summary

Literacy and instructional practices are powerful mediators of L2 learning. The ever-changing fabric of L2 learners' lives outside of the classroom have transformed classrooms into "complex communicative space[s] crisscrossed with the traces of other communicative encounters and discourses both institutional and everyday" (Baynham, 2006, p. 25). The need for pedagogies that can recruit and fully engage with L2 learners' diverse semiotic repertoires, their needs and aspirations grows as learners' lifeworlds change. The idea that there is one approach that can meet all needs is a chimera, for as the Douglas Fir Group (2016, p. 31) notes, "contexts for additional language learning can vary greatly within and across people, times, and places, and bilinguals and multilinguals will avail themselves of instruction and/or literacy to differing degrees and at different points in their learning history." What is needed is a range of well researched and well developed pedagogies that can "facilitate communication, collaboration, critical thinking, and problem-solving in linguistically and culturally diverse digital contexts (Sauro & Chapelle, 2017, p. 468).

The approaches discussed in this chapter, which are compatible with and in some cases explicitly aligned with usage-based understandings of L2 learning, can certainly benefit from additional exploration. There are other compatible instructional approaches that would as well. These include content-based approaches, genre approaches (Byrnes & Machon, 2014; Hyland, 2007), translingual approaches (García & Li, 2014), and concept-based instruction (Williams, Abraham, & Negueruela-Azarola, 2013; van Compernolle, 2011).

Implications for Understanding L2 Teaching

At the meso level of social activity, L2 learning is mediated by literacy and instructional practices. From this understanding of L2 learning, we can derive three implications for understanding L2 teaching.

1 Classrooms are significant sites of socialization and we, as teachers, are significant agents. To gain insights into the consequentiality of our roles in socializing students into their understandings of what counts as language and learning, and to be able to imagine and create new spaces for teaching and learning, we need to continuously reflect on (alone and with our students) the following features of our learning environments:
    - the spatial arrangements of our classrooms
    - our learning goals
    - the semiotic resources we use and make available to our students to use
    - the value we place on the semiotic resources our students bring to our classrooms
    - the types of instructional activities that comprise our lessons
    - the opportunities we make available to our learners to participate in them
    - our interactions with our learners
    - the ways we assess student learning.

2 The affordances of digital technologies have revolutionized literacy practices. To wit, "New orthographic and discourse conventions are proliferating, authorship is moving from individual construction to collaborative remix, and genres such as games have become canvasses for complex literacy practices" (Lotherington & Jenson, 2011, p. 227). To engage meaningfully with our students and facilitate their engagement in our learning environments we must be willing and able to weave these new literacies into our classroom practices. We must also understand that "collaborative authorship and digitally connected knowledge communities created by participatory culture" (ibid., p. 229) are now essentials to our learners' participation in social worlds outside of the classroom. We must be willing and able to integrate structures into our classrooms that accommodate these new ways of knowing and being.

3 Teaching is sophisticated, complex work. Traditionally, in many social groups and communities, teachers have worked independently. However, responding to and developing sustainable solutions for the real-world challenges of L2 teaching and learning require team efforts and collaboration. Collaborative teams of teachers work interdependently to achieve common goals. Professional collaboration recognizes that students are not the responsibility of only one teacher and that teachers need structured time to reflect on their teaching practices, problem-solve, derive new insights and understandings about teaching, and make positive sustained changes to their teaching practices.

Pedagogical Activities

This series of pedagogical activities will assist you in relating to and making sense of the concepts that inform our understanding of *L2 learning as mediated by literacy and instructional practices.*

Experiencing

A. Traditional and Digital Literacies

Work in groups of three or four to record your experiences with printed and digital texts. Printed texts include anything that is written on paper, e.g., books, newspapers, magazines, grocery lists, game instructions, and so on. Digital texts are produced through digital or electronic technology and can include texts, emails, e-library books, newspapers, magazines, and so on. Assign each group member a different colored pen or font color and record your answers on a large sheet of paper or on a digital device to which you all have access. Create two columns – DIGITAL and TRADITIONAL – and have each person list texts that he/she uses and/or produces daily.

When you complete the diagram, compare your items in each part of the diagram to your group mates' and, together, consider these questions:

- How similar/different are your items and what do you think accounts for the similarities and differences?
- What are two or three takeaways about your different literacies you gained from this activity?
- What are two or three implications you can derive for L2 teaching and learning?

B. Professional Collaboration

With a partner or in small groups, reflect on your experiences of collaborating with other teachers to discuss teaching and learning, work on shared projects, etc. If you have not yet taught, consider your experiences collaborating with your peers in your role as a student. Discuss the qualities of the experiences that you found helpful in effecting successful collaborations and those that presented difficulties, and together specify the skills and knowledge you consider to be essential for effective collaboration.

Conceptualizing

A. Concept Development

Select two of the concepts listed in Box 8.1. Craft a definition of each of the two concepts in your own words. Create one or two concrete examples of the concept that you have either experienced first-hand or can imagine. Pose one or two questions that you still have about the concept and develop a way to gather more information.

Box 8.1 Concepts: L2 learning is mediated by literacy and instructional practices

digital literacies	pedagogy of multiliteracies
funds of knowledge	scaffolding
IRF	task-based language teaching
literacies	

B. Concept Development

Choose one of the concepts you selected from the list on which to gather additional information. Using the internet, search for information on the concept. Create a list of five or so facts about it. These can include names of scholars who study the concept, studies which have been done on the concept along with their findings, visual images depicting the concept, and so on. Create a concept web that visually records the information you gathered from your explorations.

Analyzing

A. Pedagogy of Multiliteracies

Locate three studies that report on incorporating the multiliteracies approach into L2 classrooms. You can choose from studies in the reference list for this chapter or you can use your university library resources. Summarize each study (use the table in Figure 7.1, from Chapter 7) to organize the information. Share your summaries with a partner, and together consider the following questions:

- What opportunities do you think this approach offers to you, as an L2 teacher? To L2 learners?
- What challenges can you envision for incorporating this pedagogy into your own classroom or one in which you aspire to teach?
- What are two or three main points about the multiliteracies approach that you will take away from this activity?

B. Task-Based Language Teaching (TBLT)

Locate four studies that report on using the TBLT approach in L2 classrooms. Choose studies whose classroom contexts you are interested in learning more about. Summarize each study (use the table in Figure 7.1, from Chapter 7) to organize the information. Share your summaries with a partner, and together consider the following questions:

- What opportunities do you think this approach offers to you, as an L2 teacher? To L2 learners?
- What challenges can you envision for incorporating this approach into your own classroom or one in which you aspire to teach?
- What are two or three main points about the TBLT approach that you will take away from this activity?

Applying

A. Funds of Knowledge

Imagine you are teaching a class with a group of linguistically and culturally diverse students. Define the group (age, grade level, etc.) and the community in which the school is located. Develop a plan for a. gathering information on your students' funds of knowledge and b. integrating them into your teaching practices. There are several resources on the internet you might wish to consult as you develop your plan. Once developed, gather feedback on your plan from classmates, revise, and finalize by making your plan available to others, through, for example, your classroom management system, or an online open teaching forum.

B. Scaffolding

Using the same class and the plans you developed for integrating students' funds of knowledge into your teaching practices, develop a plan for scaffolding your learners into writing a research paper about one or more of their funds of knowledge. Use an internet search engine to find resources on the topic. Once completed, gather feedback on your plan from classmates, revise, and finalize by making your plan available to others, through an online open teaching forum or another public venue.

References

Ajayi, L. (2008). Meaning-making, multimodal representation, and transformative pedagogy: An exploration of meaning construction instructional practices in an ESL high school classroom. *Journal of Language, Identity & Education*, 7(3–4), 206–229.

Aljaafreh, A. (1992). *Negative feedback in second language learning and the zone of proximal development* (Unpublished Ph.D. dissertation). University of Delaware, Newark, DE.

Aljaafreh, A. & Lantolf, J. P. (1994). Negative feedback as regulation and Second Language learning in the Zone of Proximal Development. *The Modern Language Journal*, 78, 465–483.

Allen, W. H., & Paesani, K. (2010). Exploring the feasibility of a pedagogy of multiliteracies in introductory foreign language courses. *L2 Journal*, 2(1), 119–142.

Antón, M., & DiCamilla, F. (1998). Socio-cognitive functions of L1 collaborative interaction in the L2 classroom. *The Canadian Modern Language Review*, 54, 314–342.

Bartlett, L. (2007). Bilingual literacies, social identification, and educational trajectories. *Linguistics and Education*, 18(3–4), 215–231.
Barton, D., & Hamilton, M. (1998). *Local literacies: Reading and writing in one community*. London: Routledge.
Barton, D., Hamilton, M., & Ivanic, R. (Eds.) (2000). *Situated literacies: Reading and writing in context*. New York: Psychology Press.
Baynham, M. (2006). Agency and contingency in the language learning of refugees and asylum seekers. *Linguistics and Education*, 17(1), 24–39.
Bowles, M. A., & Adams, R. J. (2015). An interactionist approach to learner-learner interaction in second and foreign language classrooms. In N. Markee (Ed.), *The handbook of classroom discourse and interaction* (pp. 198–212). Malden, MA: Wiley-Blackwell.
Boxer, D., & Cortés-Conde, F. (2000). Identity and ideology: Culture and pragmatics in content-based ESL. In J. K. Hall & L. S. Verplaetse (Eds.), *Second and foreign language learning through classroom interaction* (pp. 203–219). Mahwah, NJ: Lawrence Erlbaum and Associates.
Boyd, M., & Maloof, V. M. (2000). How teachers can build on student-proposed intertextual links to facilitate student talk in the ESL classroom. In J. K. Hall & L. S. Verplaetse (Eds.), *Second and foreign language learning through classroom interaction* (pp. 163–182). Mahwah, NJ: Lawrence Erlbaum and Associates.
Breen, M., & Candlin, C. (1980). The essentials of a communicative curriculum in language teaching. *Applied Linguistics*, 1, 89–112.
Byrnes, H., & Manchón, R. M. (Eds.) (2014). *Task-based language learning: Insights from and for L2 writing* (Vol. 7). New York: John Benjamins Publishing Company.
Canagarajah, A. S. (2004). Subversive identities, pedagogical safe houses, and critical learning. In B. Norton & K. Toohey (Eds.), *Critical pedagogies and language learning* (pp.116–137). Cambridge: Cambridge University Press.
Canagarajah, A. S. (2013). Negotiating translingual literacy: An enactment. *Research in the Teaching of English*, 40–67.
Cook-Gumperz, J. (1986). Literacy and schooling: An unchanging equation. *The Social Construction of Literacy*, 16–44.
Cope, B., & Kalantzis, M. (2009). "Multiliteracies": New literacies, new learning. *Pedagogies: An International Journal*, 4(3), 164–195.
Cope, B. & Kalantiz, M. (Eds.) (2015). *A pedagogy of multiliteracies: Learning by design*. New York: Palgrave Macmillan.
Chik, A. (2014). Digital gaming and language learning: Autonomy and community. *Language Learning & Technology: A Refereed Journal for Second and Foreign Language Educators*, 18(2), 85.
Darvin, R., & Norton, B. (2015). Identity and a model of investment in applied linguistics. *Annual Review of Applied Linguistics*, 35, 36–56.
Davin, K. J., & Donato, R. (2013). Student collaboration and teacher-directed classroom dynamic assessment: A complementary pairing. *Foreign Language Annals*, 46(1), 5–22.
De Guerrero, M., & Villamil, O. S. (2000). Activating the ZPD: Mutual scaffolding in L2 peer revision. *The Modern Language Journal*, 84(1), 51–68.

DiCamilla, F. J., & Anton, M. (1997). Repetition in the collaborative discourse of L2 learners: A Vygotskian perspective. *The Canadian Modern Language Review, 53*, 609–633.

Doughty, C., & Pica, T. (1986). Information gap tasks: Do they facilitate second language acquisition? *TESOL Quarterly, 20*, 305–325.

Douglas Fir Group (2016). A transdisciplinary framework for SLA in a multilingual world. *The Modern Language Journal, 100*, 19–47.

Duff, P. A. (1995). An ethnography of communication in immersion classrooms in Hungary. *TESOL Quarterly, 29*, 505–537.

Duff, P. A. (1996). Different languages, different practices: Socialization of discourse competence in dual-language school classrooms in Hungary. In K. Bailey & D. Nunan (Eds.), *Voices from the language classroom: Qualitative research in second language education* (pp. 407–433). Cambridge: Cambridge University Press.

Duff, P. A. (2002). The discursive co-construction of knowledge, identity, and difference: An ethnography of communication in the high school mainstream. *Applied Linguistics, 23*, 289–322.

Duff, P. A. (2007). Second language socialization as sociocultural theory: Insights and issues. *Language Teaching, 40*, 309–319.

Duff, P. A. (2012). Identity, agency, and SLA. In A. Mackey & S. Gass (Eds.), *Handbook of second language acquisition* (pp. 410–426). London: Routledge.

Duff, P., & Anderson, T. (2015). Academic language and literacy socialization for second-language students. In N. Markee (Ed.), *Handbook of classroom discourse and interaction* (pp. 337–352). Malden, MA: Wiley-Blackwell.

Duff, P.A., & Kobayashi, M. (2010). The intersection of social, cognitive, and cultural processes in language learning: A second language socialization perspective. In R. Batstone (Ed.), *Sociocognitive perspectives on language use and language learning* (pp. 75–93). Oxford: Oxford University Press.

Ellis, N. C. (2002). Frequency effects in language processing: A review with implications for theories of implicit and explicit language acquisition. *Studies Second Language Acquisition, 24*(2), 143–188.

Ellis, N. C. (2008). The dynamics of second language emergence: Cycles of language use, language change, and language acquisition. *The Modern Language Journal, 92*(2), 232–249.

Ellis, R. (2003). *Task-based language learning and teaching*. Oxford: Oxford University Press.

Ellis, R. (2009). Task-based language teaching: Sorting out the misunderstandings. *International Journal of Applied Linguistics, 19*(3), 221–246.

García, O. & Li, W. (2014). *Translanguaging: Language, bilingualism, and education*. London: Palgrave Macmillan Pivot.

Gass, S. M., & Mackey, A. (2006). Input, interaction and output: An overview. *AILA Review, 19*(1), 3–17.

Gass, S., Mackey, A., & Ross-Feldman, L. (2005). Task-based interactions in classroom and laboratory settings. *Language Learning, 55*, 575–611.

Gee, J. P. (2010). A situated-sociocultural approach to literacy and technology. *The new literacies: Multiple perspectives on research and practice*, 165–193.

Gee, J. P. (2012). The old and the new in the new digital literacies. *The Educational Forum*, 76(4), 418–420.

Grabe, W., & Stoller, F. L. (2011). *Teaching and researching reading*, 2nd ed. Harlow: Pearson Education.

Grabe, W., & Zhang, C. (2016). Reading-writing relationships in first and second language academic literacy development. *Language Teaching*, 49(3), 339–355.

Gutiérrez, K. D., Baquedano-López, P., & Tejeda, C. (1999). Rethinking diversity: Hybridity and hybrid language practices in the third space. *Mind, Culture, and Activity*, 6(4), 286–303.

Hall, J. K. (1995). "Aw, man, where we goin?": Classroom interaction and the development of L2 interactional competence. *Issues in Applied Linguistics*, 6, 37–62.

Hall, J. K. (1998). Differential teacher attention to learner utterances: The construction of different opportunities for learning in the IRF. *Linguistics and Education*, 9, 287–311.

Hall, J. K. (2004). Language learning as an interactional achievement. *The Modern Language Journal*, 88, 606–612.

Hall, J. K. (2008). Language education and culture. In S. May (Ed.), *Encyclopedia of language and education (2nd ed), Volume 1* (pp. 1–11), The Netherlands: Kluwer.

Halliday, M. A. K. (1978). *Language as social semiotic*. London: Edward Arnold.

Haneda, M. (2004). The joint construction of meaning in writing conferences. *Applied Linguistics*, 25(2), 178–219.

Haneda, M. (2005). Some functions of triadic dialogue in the classroom: Examples from L2 research. *Canadian Modern Language Review*, 62(2), 313–333.

Harklau, L. (1994). Tracking and linguistic minority students: Consequences of ability grouping for second language learners. *Linguistics and Education*, 6(3), 217–244.

Harklau, L. (2002). *ESL versus mainstream classes: Contrasting L2 learning environments*. Mahwah, NJ: Erlbaum.

Harklau, L. (2007). The adolescent English language learner: Identities lost and found. In J. Cummins & C. Davison (Eds.), *The international handbook of English language teaching* (pp. 639–654). New York: Springer.

Harris, R. (2003). Language and new ethnicities: Multilingual youth and diaspora. *London: King's College Working Papers in Urban Language & Literacies*, (22).

Heath, S. B. (1983) *Ways with words: Language, life, and work in communities and in classrooms*. Cambridge: Cambridge University Press.

Hepple, E., Sockhill, M., Tan, A., & Alford, J. (2014). Multiliteracies pedagogy: Creating claymations with adolescent, post-beginner English language learners. *Journal of Adolescent and Adult Literacy*, 58(3), 219–229.

Hornberger, N. H., & Link, H. (2012). Translanguaging and transnational literacies in multilingual classrooms: A biliteracy lens. *International Journal of Bilingual Education and Bilingualism*, 15(3), 261–278.

Huang, J. (2004). Socialising ESL students into the discourse of school science through academic writing. *Language and Education*, 18(2), 97–123.

Hyland, K. (2007). Genre pedagogy: Language, literacy and L2 writing instruction. *Journal of Second Language Writing*, 16(3), 148–164.

Jewitt, C., & Kress, G. (Eds.) (2003). *Multimodal literacy*. New York: Peter Lang.

Jones, R. H., & Hafner, C. A. (2012). *Understanding digital literacies: A practical introduction*. London: Routledge.
Jonsson, C., & Muhonen, A. (2014). Multilingual repertoires and the relocalization of manga in digital media. *Discourse, Context & Media, 4*, 87–100.
Kanagy, R. (1999). Interactional routines as a mechanism for L2 acquisition and socialization in an immersion context. *Journal of Pragmatics, 31*(11), 1467–1492.
Karpov, Y. V., & Haywood, H. C. (1998). Two ways to elaborate Vygotsky's concept of mediation. *American Psychologist, 53*(1), 27.
Kenner, C., & Ruby, M. (2012). Connecting children's worlds: Creating a multilingual syncretic curriculum through partnership between complementary and mainstream schools. *Journal of Early Childhood Literacy, 13*(3), 395–417.
Kern, R. (2015). *Language, literacy, and technology*. Cambridge: Cambridge University Press.
Kim, Y. (2015). The role of tasks as vehicles for language learning in classroom interaction. In N. Markee (Ed.), *The handbook of classroom discourse and interaction* (pp. 163–181). John Wiley & Sons.
Kobayashi, M. (2006). Second language socialization through an oral project presentation: Japanese university students' experience. In G. H. Beckett & P. C. Miller (Eds.), *Project-based second and foreign language education* (pp. 71–93). Charlotte, NC: Information Age.
Kobayashi, M. (2016). L2 academic discourse socialization through oral presentations: An undergraduate student's learning trajectory in study abroad. *Canadian Modern Language Review, 72*(1), 95–121.
Koda, K. (2005). *Insights into second language reading: A cross-linguistic approach*. Cambridge: Cambridge University Press.
Kress, G. (2010). *Multimodality: A social semiotic approach to contemporary communication*. London: Routledge.
Lam, W. S. E. (2004). Border discourses and identities in transnational youth culture. In J. Mahiri (Ed.), *What they don't learn in school: Literacy in the lives of urban youth* (pp. 79–97). New York: Peter Lang Publishers.
Lam, W. S. E. (2009). Multiliteracies on instant messaging in negotiating local, translocal, and transnational affiliations: A case of an adolescent immigrant. *Reading Research Quarterly, 44*(4), 377–397.
Lankshear, C., & Knobel, M. (2011). *New literacies*. London: McGraw-Hill Education.
Lantolf, J. P., & Poehner, M. E. (2004). Dynamic assessment: Bringing the past into the future. *Applied Linguistics, 1*, 49–74.
Lantolf, J.P., & Thorne, S. L. (2006). *Sociocultural theory and the genesis of second language development*. Oxford: Oxford University Press.
Lantolf, J. P., Kurtz, L., & Kissalev, O. (2016). Understanding the revolutionary character of L2 development in the ZPD: Why levels of mediation matter. *Language and Sociocultural Theory, 3*(2), 153–171.
Lee, J. S., & Bucholtz, M. (2015). Language socialization across learning spaces. In N. Markee (Ed.), *The handbook of classroom discourse and interaction* (pp. 319–336). Malden, MA: Wiley-Blackwell.
Lee, Y. A. (2007). Third turn position in teacher talk: Contingency and the work of teaching. *Journal of Pragmatics, 39*(6), 1204–1230.

Lin, A. (1999a). Resistance and creativity in English reading lessons in Hong Kong. *Language, Culture and Curriculum, 12*, 285–296.

Lin, A. (1999b). Doing-English: Lessons in the reproduction or transformation of social worlds? *TESOL Quarterly, 33*, 393–412.

Long, M. (2014). *Second language acquisition and task-based language teaching*. John Wiley & Sons.

Long, M., & Crookes, G. (1993). Units of analysis in syllabus design: The case for task. In G. Crookes & S. Gass (Eds.), *Tasks in pedagogical contexts* (pp. 9–54). Clevedon: Multilingual Matters.

Lotherington, H. (2012). *Pedagogy of multiliteracies: Rewriting goldilocks*. London: Routledge.

Lotherington, H., & Jenson, J. (2011). Teaching multimodal and digital literacy in L2 settings: New literacies, new basics, new pedagogies. *Annual Review of Applied Linguistics, 31*, 226–246.

Martin-Jones, M., & Bhatt, A. (1998). Literacies in the lives of young Gujarati speakers in Leicester. In L. Verhoeven & A. Y. Durgunoglu (Eds.), *Literacy development in a multilingual context* (pp. 37–50). Mahwah, NJ: Lawrence Erlbaum.

Maybin, J. (2008). Revoicing across learning spaces. In N. Hornberger (Ed.), *Encyclopedia of language and education* (pp. 837–848). New York: Springer.

McCarty, T., & Watahomigie, L. (1998). Language and literacy in American Indian and Alaska native communities. In B. Perez (Ed.), *Sociocultural contexts of language and literacy* (pp. 69–98). Mahwah, NJ: Lawrence Erlbaum.

McCormick, D., & Donato, R. (2000). Teacher question as scaffolding assistance in an ESL classroom. In J. K. Hall & L. Verplaetse (Eds.), *Second and foreign language learning through classroom interaction* (pp. 183–203). Mahwah, NJ: Erlbaum.

McGinnis, T., Goodstein-Stolzenberg, A., & Saliani, E. C. (2007). "indnpride": Online spaces of transnational youth as sites of creative and sophisticated literacy and identity work. *Linguistics and Education, 18*(3–4), 283–304.

Mehan, H., & Griffin, P. (1980). Socialization: The view from classroom interactions. *Sociological Inquiry, 50*(3–4), 357–392.

Miller, E. R., & Zuengler, J. (2011). Negotiating access to learning through resistance to classroom practice. *The Modern Language Journal, 95*(s1), 130–147.

Minick, N. (1987). The development of Vygotsky's thought: An introduction. In *The collected works of LS Vygotsky* (pp. 17–36). Boston, MA: Springer.

Moje, E. B., Ciechanowski, K. M., Kramer, K., Ellis, L., Carrillo, R., & Collazo, T. (2004). Working toward third space in content area literacy: An examination of everyday funds of knowledge and discourse. *Reading Research Quarterly, 39*(1), 38–70.

Moll, L., Amanti, C., Neff, D., & González, N. (1992). Funds of knowledge for teaching: Using a qualitative approach to connect homes and classrooms. *Theory into Practice, 31*, 132–141.

Moll, L., Amanti, C., Neff, D., & Gonzalez, N. (2005). Funds of knowledge for teaching: Using a qualitative approach to connect homes and classrooms. In N. Gonzalez, L. Moll, & C. Amanti (Eds.), *Funds of knowledge: Theorizing practices in households, communities, and classrooms* (pp. 71–87). Mahwah, NJ: Lawrence Erlbaum and Associates.

Mondada, L., & Pekarek, S. (2004). Second language acquisition as situated practice: Task accomplishment in the French second language classroom. *The Modern Language Journal, 88*, 501–518.

Moore, L. C. (1999). Language socialization research and French language education in Africa: A Cameroonian case study. *Canadian Modern Language Review, 52*, 329–350.

Moore, L. C. (2017). Multilingual socialization and education in non-Western settings. In P. A. Duff & S. May (Eds.), *Language socialization: Encyclopedia of language and education* (pp. 155–168). New York: Springer.

Morita, N. 2000. Discourse socialization through oral classroom activities in a TESL graduate program. *TESOL Quarterly, 34*, 279–310.

Morita, N. (2004). Negotiating participation and identity in second language academic communities. *TESOL Quarterly, 38*, 573–603.

Nassaji, H., & Wells, G. (2000). What's the use of "Triadic Dialogue"?: An investigation of teacher–student interaction. *Applied Linguistics, 21*, 376–406.

New London Group. (1996). A pedagogy of multiliteracies: Designing social futures. *Harvard Educational Review, 66*, 60–92.

Ohta, A. S. (1999). Interactional routines and the socialization of interactional style in adult learners of Japanese. *Journal of Pragmatics, 31*(11), 1493–1512.

Ortlieb, E., & Cheek Jr, E. H. (Eds.) (2017). *Addressing diversity in literacy instruction*. Bingley: Emerald Publishing Limited.

Pahl, K. (2014). *Materializing literacies in communities: The uses of literacy revisited*. London: Bloomsbury Publishing.

Phillips, S. (1983). *The invisible culture: Communication in classroom and community in the Warm Springs Indian reservation*. White Plains, NY: Longman.

Poole, D. (1992). Language socialization in the second language classroom. *Language Learning, 42*, 593–616.

Prabhu, N. S. (1987). *Second language pedagogy*. Oxford: Oxford University Press.

Reinhardt, J., & Thorne, S. L. (2017). Language socialization in digital contexts. In P. A. Duff & S. May (Eds.), *Language socialization. Encyclopedia of language and education*, 3rd ed. (pp. 1–13). Cham: Springer.

Robinson, P. (2001) Task complexity, task difficulty, and task production: Exploring interactions in a componential framework. *Applied Linguistics, 22*, 27–57.

Sauro, S., & Chapelle, C. A. (2017). Toward langua-technocultural competence. In C. A. Chapelle & S. Sauro (Eds.), *The handbook of technology and second language teaching and learning* (pp. 459–472). John Wiley & Sons.

Seloni, L. (2011). Academic literacy socialization of first year doctoral students in US: A micro-ethnographic perspective. *English for Specific Purposes, 31*, 47–59.

Seloni, L. (2014). "I'm an artist and a scholar who is trying to find a middle point": A textographic analysis of a Colombian art historian's thesis writing. *Journal of Second Language Writing, 25*, 79–99.

Schleppegrell, M. J. (2013). The role of metalanguage in supporting academic language development. *Language Learning, 63*(1), 153–170.

Schmidt, R. (1990). The role of consciousness in second language learning. *Applied Linguistics, 11*, 129–158.

Scollon, R., & Scollon, S. B. (1981). *Narrative, literacy, and face in interethnic communication.* New York: Ablex Publishing Corporation.

Skehan, P. (1996). A framework for the implementation of task-based instruction. *Applied Linguistics, 17,* 38–62.

Smythe, S., & Toohey, K. (2009). Bringing home and community to school: Institutional constraints and pedagogic possibilities. In J. Miller, A. Kostogriz, & M. Gearon (Eds.), *Culturally and linguistically diverse classrooms: New dilemmas for teachers* (pp. 273–290). Clevedon: Multilingual Matters.

Steinkuehler, C. A. (2008). Cognition and literacy in massively multiplayer online games. In J. Coiro, M. Knobel, C., Lankshear & D. Leu (Eds.), *Handbook of research on new literacies* (pp. 611–634). Mahwah: Lawrence Erlbaum and Associates.

Stone, C. A. (1998). Should we salvage the scaffolding metaphor? *Journal of Learning Disabilities, 31,* 409–413.

Tarone, E., & Bigelow, M. (2005). Impact of literacy on oral language processing: Implications for SLA research. *Annual Review of Applied Linguistics, 25,* 77–97.

Tarone, E., Bigelow, M., & Hansen, K. (2009). *Literacy and oracy in second language acquisition.* Oxford: Oxford University Press.

Talmy, S. (2008). The cultural productions of the ESL student at Tradewinds High: Contingency, multidirectionality, and identity in L2 socialization. *Applied Linguistics, 29*(4), 619–644.

Thorne, S. L. (2008). Transcultural communication in open internet environments and massively multiplayer online games. *Mediating Discourse Online,* 305.

Thorne, S. L., Fischer, I., & Lu, X. (2012). The semiotic ecology and linguistic complexity of an online game world. *ReCALL, 24*(3), 279–301.

Toohey, K. (1998). "Breaking them up, taking them away": Constructing ESL students in grade one. *TESOL Quarterly, 32,* 61–84.

Toohey, K., Day, E. & Manyak, P. (2007). ESL learners in the early school years: Identity and mediated classroom practices. In J. Cummins & C. Davison (Eds.), *International handbook of English language teaching* (pp. 625–638). Springer.

van Compernolle, R.A. (2011). Developing second language sociopragmatic knowledge through concept-based instruction: A microgenetic case study. *Journal of Pragmatics, 43,* 3267–3283.

Vickers, C. (2007). Second language socialization through team interaction among electrical and computer engineering students. *The Modern Language Journal, 91,* 621–640.

Vygotsky, L. S. (1978). *Mind in society.* Cambridge, MA: Harvard University Press.

Vygotsky, L. S. (1981). The genesis of higher mental functions. In J. V. Wertsch (Ed.), *The concept of activity in Soviet psychology* (pp. 144–188). Armonk, NY: M. E. Sharpe.

Waring, H. Z. (2008). Using explicit positive assessment in the language classroom: IRF, feedback, and learning opportunities. *The Modern Language Journal, 92*(4), 577–594.

Waring, H. Z. (2009). Moving out of IRF: A single case analysis. *Language Learning, 59*(4), 796–824.

Warriner, D. S. (2007). Transnational literacies: Immigration, language learning, and identity. *Linguistics and Education, 18*(3), 201–214.

Wells, G. (1993) Reevaluating the IRF sequence: A proposal for the articulation of theories of activity and discourse for the analysis of teaching and learning in the classroom. *Linguistics and Education, 5*, 1–38.

Willett, J. (1995). Becoming first graders in an L2: An ethnographic study of L2 socialization. *TESOL Quarterly, 29*, 473–503.

Williams, L., Abraham, L. B., & Negueruela-Azarola, E. (2013). Using concept-based instruction in the L2 classroom: Perspectives from current and future language teachers. *Language Teaching Research, 17*(3), 363–381.

Wood, D., Bruner, J. S., & Ross, G. (1976). The role of tutoring in problem solving. *Journal of Child Psychology & Psychiatry & Allied Disciplines, 17*(2), 89–100.

Yang, L. (2010). Doing a group presentation: Negotiations and challenges experienced by five Chinese ESL students of commerce at a Canadian university. *Language Teaching Research, 14*(2), 141–160.

Young-Scholten, M. (2013). Low-educated immigrants and the social relevance of second language acquisition research. *Second Language Research, 29*(4), 441–454.

Zapata, G. C., & Lacorte, M. (2018). *Multiliteracies pedagogy and language learning.*

Zappa-Hollman, S. (2007). Academic presentations across post-secondary contexts: The discourse socialization of non-native English speakers. *Canadian Modern Language Review, 6*(4), 455–485.

Zappa-Hollman, S., & Duff, P. A. (2014). Academic English socialization through individual networks of practice. *TESOL Quarterly, 49*(2), 333–368.

Zentella, A. C. (1997). *Growing up bilingual.* Oxford: Blackwell.

Chapter 9

L2 Learning Is Mediated by Language Ideologies

Overview

At the macro level of social activity are large-scale, society-wide ideologies about languages. These ideologies are highly significant to L2 learning as they mediate decision making in educational institutions, and thereby shape the types of language education approaches that are offered, the languages of instruction and even the terms used to refer to L2 learners. They also influence people's decisions to study additional languages, their choices for which languages they want to learn and the degree of agency they have in making those choices, and their investments in and motivations for seeking out opportunities to use the target languages and develop relationships with speakers of the languages (Douglas Fir Group, 2016). In this chapter, we examine more closely the role that language ideologies play in mediating L2 learning.

Language Ideologies

We all hold beliefs about language in general and about specific languages in particular. Beliefs are assumptions or suppositions about ideas, concepts, people, things, events, and so on that we take to be true. We may think that a particular language sounds more sophisticated than others, or that one language is more complicated or difficult to learn than another. We also hold beliefs about individuals and social groups who are users of those languages. For example, we may think that some people's ways of using what we consider to be "our language" are inappropriate or lazy or that a language spoken by people we believe to be cultured is itself a cultured entity.

Such normative beliefs constitute language ideologies (Irvine & Gal, 2000; Kroskrity, 2004; Piller, 2015; Woolard & Schieffelin, 1994). Language ideologies are explicit and implicit "sets of beliefs about language articulated by users as a rationalization or justification of perceived language structure and use" (Silverstein, 1979, p. 193). We construct and share our ideologies with members of our social groups, communities, and institutions. We use them to justify or rationalize decisions about language behavior and the social value of people and social groups who are linked to different varieties of language.

While to some, ideologies may appear to be commonsense, unbiased views of the relative value of languages, in fact they are rooted in and responsive to the interests of social groups with high levels of power and prestige (Blommaert & Rampton, 2011; Wiley, 2014; Woolard, 1990). There is nothing inherent in a language that gives it a certain standing, makes it better, more linguistically correct, or more able to express social or intellectual ideas than other languages. Languages acquire their prestige when their speakers have prestige (Milroy, 2001). Language ideologies, then, are social constructs that serve moral and political ends. Like all social constructs, language ideologies are not monolithic but are multiple and contested (Piller, 2015). A number of language ideologies are of particular relevance to L2 learning. We examine these in the next sections.

Ideology of Standard Language

The *standard language ideology* is the belief that one variety of a language is superior to other coexisting ones. This variety is the language used by the most powerful groups in society. It is the variety that is used in governments, taught in schools, and codified in dictionaries and prescriptive grammar books that set out rules governing how a language variety should and should not be used. It is predicated on an ideology of language as an objective and stable entity. Sinfree Makoni and Alastair Pennycook (2007) explain further in Quote 9.1.

Quote 9.1 The Ideology of Language

The concept of language, and indeed the 'metadiscursive regimes' used to describe languages are firmly located in Western linguistic and cultural suppositions. They do not describe any real state of affairs in the world, i.e. they are not natural kinds (Danzinger, 1997): they are convenient fictions only to the extent that they provide a useful way of understanding the world and shaping language users, and they are very inconvenient fictions to the extent that they produce particular and limiting views on how language operates in the world.

Makoni and Pennycook (2007, p. 27)

A component of the standard language ideology is the belief in uniformity of use across speakers of the standard variety. In the case of English, for example, each separate world variety of it, such as American English, British English, and Australian English, is considered to be a standard variety of English and, thus, to be stable and uniform. Uses of it and the people who use it are judged to be correct and proper. Variation in the use of the standard is considered to be deviant, "the contingent and deplorable result of some users' carelessness, idleness or incompetence" (Cameron, 1995, p. 39). Uses of other varieties and their users are judged against the standard and stigmatized as improper and even unintelligent. In this way, the standard language ideology serves to justify social inequalities.

The standard language ideology is a feature of national political discourse; in many nations, their standard languages are considered to be the only appropriate medium for use in education, the workplace, government, and the media (Simpson & Whiteside, 2015). An example of the standard language ideology is the widespread belief in the United States in Standard American English (SAE) as the ideal version of American English. Many other varieties of American English exist including African American English, Southern English, and Southwestern English. These varieties are recognized as dialects. Dialects are language varieties that are associated with groups of people from particular geographic regions, particular ethnic groups, and particular socioeconomic groups. It is not that the structural properties of SAE are inherently better than those of other varieties of American English. Rather, it is SAE's association with the dominant social groups of the US that gives it its privileged status. The ideology of a standard language shapes the practices of social institutions and their members' beliefs and attitudes about the use of the standard. For example, it is used to restrict the use of learners' home languages in educational systems (Makoni & Pennycook, 2012). In L2 classrooms it is used to exclude L2 learners' use of their L1s and to justify preoccupations with error correction and attributions of identities to L2 learners as deficient communicators (Gorter & Cenoz, 2017).

Ideology of Monolingualism

An equally pervasive ideology is the *ideology of monolingualism* (Farr & Song, 2011; Flores, 2013). Monolingualism refers to the condition of being able to speak only one standard language. Despite the fact that most of the world's inhabitants are bilingual, monolingualism is often regarded as the natural human condition, and bilingualism and multilingualism as deviations. This ideology has its roots in the development of the Western European nation-state, which presented "one nation – one language" as the political ideal. This ideology is connected to other beliefs about national identity, such as the belief that "the nation state should be as homogeneous as possible, and that a dimension of that homogeneity is monolingualism (Simpson & Whiteside, 2015, p. 371).

The ideology of monolingualism is a common belief in the United States, and in fact is considered to be a chief characteristic of American citizenship, despite "*ongoing* multilingual and multicultural 'super-diversity'" (Wiley, 2014, p. 28, emphasis in original). While monolingualism is celebrated, language diversity is often seen as an unfortunate result of immigration, and thus not well tolerated, "except perhaps on special ethnic holidays when it is considered appropriate to celebrate diversity" (Wiley & Lukes, 1996, p. 520). The consequences of such an ideology at the national level include the insistence of linguistic assimilation for all groups and the development of standard language policies at local and state levels that preclude the use of other varieties. In schools, the ideology leads to a devaluation of the language varieties that students bring with them and, in many cases, of the students themselves (Rojo, 2015).

Ideology of the Native Speaker

Alongside the belief in monolingualism is the ideology of the *monolingual native speaker*. The term "native speaker" refers to a language user who is a member of a monolingual community of standard language users and who is imaged to possess an ideal state of linguistic competence (Ortega, 2013). In the case of English, "native English speakers" are those who learn English as their first language in countries that are associated with the standard varieties of their countries (Shuck, 2006). The term "nonnative English speaker" is used to refer to everyone else regardless of how they learned English or how extensive their repertoires are. A component of this ideology is the belief that multilingualism is plural monolingualism, with the languages existing in the minds of individuals as distinct and autonomous systems (Makoni & Pennycook, 2012).

The ideology of a monolingual native speaker has had a particularly negative influence on the agendas of SLA research around the world. Despite substantial evidence revealing the dynamic, diverse, and adaptable nature of individual language knowledge, much SLA research continues to rely on "the monolingual native speaker's idealized competence as a benchmark for defining and evaluating L2 learning" (Douglas Fir Group, 2016, p. 35). The same ideology has had a negative effective on language education programs as they continue to rely on the construct of a monolingual native speaker in designing curriculum, instruction, and assessment tools (ibid.). The *native speaker fallacy* (Phillipson, 1992), which suggests that the ideal language teacher is a native speaker of the target language, also remains prominent in language teacher preparation programs and hiring practices.

Language Policy and Planning

Language ideologies influence language policy and planning on all levels of social activity. Language planning refers to measures taken "to influence the behaviors of others with respect to the acquisition, structure, or functional allocation of their language codes" (Cooper, 1989, p. 45). Language planning can take place in any social group in any social institution, such as schools, workplaces, religious centers, community organizations, and even families.

Language policies establish and regulate the rights of individuals and groups to use and maintain particular language varieties. They involve decision making, formally and informally, at the national, state, community, and individual levels. Decisions include determining which language variety or varieties are standard and official, how they are to be used in community settings, and the types of educational opportunities individuals have to learn, use, and maintain them (Douglas Fir Group, 2016; Farr & Song, 2011).

Language policies vary in terms of degree of explicitness. They can be stated explicitly in official documents, government documents, laws, and educational guidelines. They can also be displayed on public and commercial signs. One example of an explicit language policy for a small business was created by a business owner of a restaurant in a city located in the northeastern part of the United States. The sign read in part *This is AMERICA, when ordering "SPEAK ENGLISH"*. The sign adorned the window of the business for at least ten years, until 2016 when the business changed hands and the new owner removed it.

Language policies can also be implicit, embedded and observed in institutional practices. For example, although there is no official national policy making English the language of government in the United States, all official government activities are conducted in English. As another example, while there is no official policy about language use in schools at the state or national levels, nonstandard varieties of English are often excluded from use as medium of instruction. This is despite clear evidence that use of nonstandard varieties has a positive effect not only on students' acquisition of standard varieties, but also on their participation, performance on standardized tests, and overall academic achievement (Tollefson, 2017). As a final example, while there is no explicit language policy for families, family members choose to use specific language varieties with their children and other family members. In some families it may be the variety that they believe holds the greatest value for their children; other families may decide to use two languages: a heritage language and a standard variety of their community language.

Implicit language policies can become hegemonic. Hegemony refers to the "ability of dominant groups to maintain and exercise power either through coercion or by the manufacture of consent" (Wiley, 1996, p. 113). Linguistic hegemony occurs when those in power are able to get those with less power to accept their language norms as standard. Schools are principal instruments in "promoting a consensus regarding the alleged superiority of standardized languages" (ibid.)

Language Education Policies

Language policies serve as a central gatekeeper to education (McCarty, 2003; Tollefson & Tsui, 2014). They impact curricula decisions, instructional practices, and even teaching materials. One of the more significant policies related to L2 learning has to do with the *medium of instruction*. Choices about languages of instruction are not simply about the efficiency of one language variety over another. Choices have to do with equitable access to educational opportunities and, more generally, with "struggles for political and economic participation, democracy, and human rights" (McCarty, 2003, p. 72). Tsui and Tollefson (2003) elaborate on the power embodied in the medium of instruction in Quote 9.2.

Quote 9.2 Medium of Instruction

Medium of instruction is the most powerful means of maintaining and revitalizing a language and a culture; it is the most important form of intergenerational transmission (Fishman & Fishman, 2000). It is also the most direct agent of linguistic genocide (Skutnabb-Kangas, 2000, 2002). Medium-of-instruction policy determines which social and linguistic groups have access to political and economic opportunities, and which groups are disenfranchised. It is therefore a key means of power (re)distribution and social (re)construction, as well as a key arena in which political conflicts among countries and ethnolinguistic, social and political groups are realized.

Tsui & Tollefson (2003, p. 2)

Choices of languages of instruction are complex. We know that the use of learners' language varieties in learning, especially in the primary years has long-term benefits for learners' academic performance. We also know that learners must have opportunities to learn the languages that are necessary for higher education and employment. Even with policies that support equity and access to these learning opportunities, there is often a gap between official policies and everyday practices (Tollefson & Tsui, 2003). Some of the challenges that local programs face include lack of resources, such as teaching materials and trained teachers, and inadequate funds. Further complicating the issue of equitable access to educational opportunities are social changes brought about by globalization. According to Tollefson and Tsui (2014), two changes have been the significant migration of labor from rural areas to cities and the creation of new types of work in, for example, business and finance, service industries, and government agencies, many of which require command of dominant languages such as English and Chinese. These changes have resulted in increased demand for workers with at least secondary education and with literacy skills in one or more of the dominant languages. The new types of work and their language demands have major consequences for educational language policies, and in particular for decisions about the languages of instruction in schools, resulting in ever-increasing pressure to use the dominant languages in schools to teach the basic curriculum.

Language Education Programs

Bilingual education programs are a standard means of providing equity and access to learning opportunities for linguistically diverse groups around the world. Bilingual education involves using two languages to teach school subjects. One is the learners' native language and the other language is typically a dominant language such as English, with varying amounts of each language used in accordance with the program model. The Council of Europe, an international organization whose aim is to uphold democracy and protect human rights, undertook a major effort with respect to bilingual/multilingual education in Europe shortly after the turn into the twenty-first century. One implementation of its language education policies (see Quote 9.2) has been the development of the *Common European Framework of Reference for Languages* (CEFRL) (Council of Europe, 2001). Created to facilitate clarity and comparability in language education programs, CEFRL is a set of standards and guidelines for language programs that are specifically for the development of language curricula, the design of teaching and learning materials, and the assessment of language proficiency.

CEFRL is widely used in many education systems as a tool for language policy and language assessment, not only in Europe but in countries around the world as well (Gorter & Cenoz, 2016). This acceptance notwithstanding, the resource is not without its critics. Perhaps the most significant criticism has to do with the traditional views of language and

> **Quote 9.3 The Council of Europe Language Education Policies**
>
> Council of Europe language education policies aim to promote:
>
> PLURILINGUALISM: all are entitled to develop a degree of communicative ability in a number of languages over their lifetime in accordance with their needs
>
> LINGUISTIC DIVERSITY: Europe is multilingual and all its languages are equally valuable modes of communication and expressions of identity; the right to use and to learn one's language(s) is protected in Council of Europe Conventions
>
> MUTUAL UNDERSTANDING: the opportunity to learn other languages is an essential condition for intercultural communication and acceptance of cultural differences
>
> DEMOCRATIC CITIZENSHIP: participation in democratic and social processes in multilingual societies is facilitated by the plurilingual competence of individuals
>
> SOCIAL COHESION: equality of opportunity for personal development, education, employment, mobility, access to information and cultural enrichment depends on access to language learning throughout life.
>
> Retrieved from www.coe.int/t/dg4/linguistic/
Division_EN.asp January 22, 2018

learning that undergird the framework. According to Blommaert and Backus (2011, p. 4), the concern is this:

> In spite of significant advances in the field of language knowledge, and in spite of the increasing complexity of superdiverse sociolinguistic environments, dominant discourses on this topic seem to increasingly turn to entirely obsolete and conclusively discredited models of language knowledge. The European Common Framework for Languages [sic] is naturally the most outspoken case, but *language and literacy testing methods predicated on linear and uniform 'levels' of knowledge and developmental progression* are back in force.
>
> (emphasis added)

The United States has a long history of bilingual education programs in different forms. *Transitional bilingual education program*s are meant to transition learners who do not speak American English into English academic language development. Students begin taking a few subjects in their first languages and others in American English. Over time, they move to instruction in English for all subjects. In *dual language* or *two-way bilingual education programs* L2 learners and American English-speaking students are integrated with the goal of developing academic language skills in both languages in both groups of learners. However, explicit language education policies such as those of the Council of Europe do not exist at the national level. Decisions about types of programs, curricular and instructional practices, teaching materials, and assessment practices are made at the local and state levels.

Regardless of the type, traditional bilingual education programs have been similarly criticized for treating language knowledge as static and homogeneous, and keeping the two languages separate, independent from each other so as not to "'contaminate' the other named language" (Otheguy, García & Reid, 2015, p. 302; Flores & García, 2017; García & Sylvan, 2011). Cummins and Swain (1986, p. 108) have referred to this implicit language policy as "bilingualism through monolingualism". Gorter and Cenoz (2017) argue that these same views on language continue to be strong in other bilingual education contexts such as Canadian immersion programs, the programs of the Basque country of Spain, and elsewhere.

As we have discussed in earlier chapters, usage-based understandings of language and learning have significantly undercut such views on language and the ideologies of standard language and the monolingual native speaker underpinning them. Also undercutting them is a growing number of studies documenting how people make use of the various multilingual resources of their repertoires in their everyday practices. These efforts have given rise to spaces for the investigation and development of approaches to teaching that are "more suited to the realities of [L2 learners'] lives in superdiverse, multilingual neighborhoods and workplaces" (Simpson & Whiteside, 2015, p. 377), and thus reflect shifting language ideologies.

One example of an emerging pedagogy is the *translanguaging approach*. Translanguaging has become a common term to refer to people's flexible, fluid use of their multilingual resources to communicate with others in specific contexts of action (see Chapter 2; Creese & Blackledge, 2010, 2014; García & Leiva, 2014; García & Li, 2014; Otheguy, García & Reid, 2015). Its conceptualization of language marks an ideological shift away from a focus on languages as fixed, discrete systems, and bilingualism and multilingualism as knowledge of separate language systems. It is grounded on a view of language as ever-evolving constellations of social constructions (re)created for the purpose of making meaning. A translanguaging pedagogy is a new type of bilingual education program that seeks to recruit all of the learners' linguistic and other semiotic resources at their disposal such that they are able to engage actively and critically in the contexts of action comprising their classroom communities and thereby maximize their academic achievements (Creese & Blackledge, 2010, 2015; García & Li, 2014; García & Kano, 2014). García and Kanno (2014, p. 275) explain further:

> In a translanguaging classroom, by rejecting the subjugation of one language to the other and giving agency to bilingual students to self-regulate their language practices in learning, diverse linguistic and cultural repertoires are harnessed to their fullest extent. Through those experiences, bilingual students can construct truly bilingual identities and enrich their languaging and academic experiences.

The goals of a translanguaging pedagogy as set out by Ofelia García and Li Wei are stated in Quote 9.4. What makes the translanguaging approach different from other bilingual education approaches is that it is meant to be transformative, that is, to position L2 learners as creative and competent, able to bring different dimensions of their life experiences together to create new voices, new identities, and new social realities.

Quote 9.4 Goals of Translanguaging Pedagogy

To differentiate among students' levels and adapt instruction to different types of students in multilingual classrooms.

To build background knowledge so that students can make meaning of the content being taught and of the ways of languaging in the lesson.

To deepen understandings and sociopolitical engagement, develop and extend new knowledge, and develop critical thinking and critical consciousness.

For cross-linguistic metalinguistic awareness so as to strengthen the students' ability to meet the communicative exigencies of the socioeducational situation.

For cross-linguistic flexibility so as to use language practices competently. For identity investment and positionality; that is, to engage learners.

To interrogate linguistic inequality and disrupt linguistic hierarchies and social structures.

Garcia & Li (2014, p. 121)

Summary

Whether we are conscious of them or not, we all hold beliefs about language, about learning, and about ourselves and others as language users and learners. Our ideologies permeate every action we take, "enacted as common sense rationality that is actively practiced and ongoingly reconstituted in social interaction ... as practical discursive methods for sense-making, rationalizing ... providing evidence among many others" (Miller, 2014, p. 122).

Three ideologies in particular are especially influential to L2 teaching and learning experiences, shaping decision making at all levels of social activity: the standard language ideology, the ideology of monolingualism, and the native speaker ideology. These ideologies are inextricably connected to not only explicit, overt language and language education policies but also to implicit, unofficial, grassroots policies. While the ideologies may present some challenges to designing and implementing L2 teaching practices that provide relevant language learning experiences, they are not static or monolithic; they can be contested and changed. Recent advances in pedagogical approaches based on concepts such as translanguaging that reflect current understandings of language and learning are a case in point; they hold great promise for transforming language education policies at all levels of social activity.

Implications for Understanding L2 Teaching

From an understanding of L2 learning as mediated by language ideologies, we can derive three implications for understanding L2 teaching.

1 Our beliefs about language and learning mediate every decision we make as language teachers. The decisions we make and the actions we take regarding curricular content, resources, instructional activities, and assessment measures as well as regarding the language(s) we use in the classroom and allow the students to use are all are informed by our ideologies, no matter how unaware we may be of our beliefs. Also affecting our decisions and actions are the language ideologies expressed in the policies of our educational institutions. To be agentive in our work as L2 teachers requires at the minimum developing a critical awareness of our beliefs and those of the larger institutional contexts in which we teach and of how they influence our actions as teachers, the kinds of learning environments we create in our classrooms, and the relationships we develop with students, colleagues, and administrators. Such enhanced

understandings will facilitate our crafting of actions that respond strategically to the possibilities and limitations of our particular teaching contexts in light of our past experiences and future goals (Haneda & Sherman, 2016).
2   L2 teachers play an instrumental role in (re)creating language policies in our professional practices. A significant means by which we do this is through the words we use to refer to L2 learners in our interactions, both oral and written, with colleagues and administrators. Words are powerful resources. Words may not change reality, but they can change how people perceive reality. Labels and terms such as *nonnative*, *deficient*, and *remedial* mark L2 learners as incomplete, lacking something. They render invisible the knowledge and skills that L2 learners have already accumulated in their life experiences and can even lead to unwanted or harmful consequences. Even the term *language* calls to mind an objective, static system. Together, these and other similar terms reinforce language ideologies of the native speaker and monolingualism.

One way to counteract these ideologies is to create a "personal" language policy to be mindful of the words we use and to encourage others in our schools to do the same in both official and unofficial interactions. Actions we can take include omitting words such as *deficient* and *remedial* in descriptions of courses or programs at our schools; trading out *nonnative* for *multilingual* in our descriptions of our learners and exchanging *language* for the term *semiotic repertoires* to describe course content, the focus of our instructional practices, and the objects of L2 learning. Providing explanations for our word choices to our students, colleagues, and administrators and to parents and other stakeholders can help to create more informed understandings of the multilingual worlds in which we live and the need for pedagogical approaches like the translanguaging approach.
3   In addition to generating change through the words we use, we need to be mindful of the learning environments we create in our classrooms. We can begin by imagining learning environments where translanguaging is the norm, where our students' semiotic resources and skills are not erased, but are explored and drawn on, where learning opportunities allow for a range of modalities in meaning making, opening up new "expressive potentials" (Cope & Kalantzis, 2009, p. 188) for learners; where learning experiences involve a variety of knowledge processes and a variety of learning spaces; where learners are able to imagine, refashion or take on new identities; and where learners as meaning-makers are acknowledged as designers of their social futures (Cope & Kalantzis, 2002).

Pedagogical Activities

This series of pedagogical activities will assist you in relating to and making sense of the concepts that inform our understanding of *L2 learning as mediated by language ideologies.*

Experiencing

A. Language Ideologies

With a partner or small group, consider the following questions:

- What are your beliefs about language in general? About the languages you speak? About languages spoken by others in your community?
- Do you feel that some languages are privileged over other languages in your community? If yes, how so? If no, support your response with a few examples from your own experiences.
- Have your beliefs changed as you have progressed through your preparation to become an L2 teacher? If yes, how so? If no, please explain.
- Should L2 teachers play an active role in promoting ideologies of linguistic diversity and translanguaging versus ideologies of monolingualism and a standard language? If yes, how? If no, please explain.

B. The Ideology of Native Speaking L2 Teacher

With a partner or small group, consider the following: rightly or wrongly, the ideal of a native speaking L2 teacher continues to thrive as "a model, a norm and a goal" (Creese, Blackledge, & Takhi, 2014, p. 938) in the L2 teaching profession. Reflect on the identities of teachers of the languages you studied in your educational program over the years. Were they native or nonnative speakers of the target languages? Do you feel that these identities made a difference in how they taught? In how you learned? Now that you are or are becoming an L2 teacher, consider the advantages and disadvantages of learning from monolingual speakers of the target language and from multilingual speakers of the target language. What implications can you derive from your considerations for your own teaching practices?

Conceptualizing

A. Concept Development

Select two of the concepts listed in Box 9.1. Craft a definition of each of the two concepts in your own words. Create one or two concrete examples of the concept that you have either experienced first-hand or can imagine. Pose one or two questions that you still have about the concept and develop a way to gather more information.

> **Box 9.1 Concepts: L2 learning is mediated by language ideologies**
>
> Common European Framework of Reference for Languages
> dual language education programs
> ideologies
> language education policies
> language policies
> medium of instruction
> monolingualism ideology
> monolingual native speaker ideology
> standard language ideology
> translanguaging pedagogy
> transitional bilingual education programs

B. Concept Development

Choose one of the concepts you selected from the list on which to gather additional information. Using the internet, search for information on the concept. Create a list of five or so facts about it. These can include names of scholars who study the concept, studies that have been done on the concept along with their findings, visual images depicting the concept, and so on. Create a concept web that visually records the information you gathered from your explorations.

Analyzing

A. Linguistic Landscapes

Linguistic landscape refers to the "visibility and salience of languages on public and commercial signs in a given territory or region" (Landry & Bourhis, 1997, p. 23). Conducting a study of a linguistic landscape of a particular public space indicates which language(s) are prominent and valued. Conduct a linguistic landscape of your community by collecting representative samples of the language(s) that appear in public places, taking photographs of the representations, and noting where each is located. Consider street signs, billboards, graffiti, posters on poles, lampposts and hanging on walls, commercial signs, shop windows, posted menus, street names, place names, and so on.

Once you have collected your data, create a table indicating a. whether the representation is top-down (government-related, official signs) or bottom-up (non-official, related to businesses, private organizations or persons), b. type of representation (e.g., graffiti, menu), and 3. the language(s) featured. Then, consider the following questions:

- What patterns in use of languages and types of representation can you detect within and across top-down and bottom-up signs?
- For top-down signs, what policies on language do they appear to support?
- For bottom-up signs, what views on language do they appear to support?
- What can you conclude about the relationship between language policies, language ideologies, and linguistic landscapes?

C. Language Policies

Find two articles on national language education policies, each of which reports on a particular geographical area in which you have interest. For some background information, you may wish to consult the website of the *International Network for Language Education Policy Studies* (INLEPS), an association of scholars and researchers, at www.language educationpolicy.org. Write a paper in which you a. summarize each study's findings, b. compare findings across contexts, and c. discuss what you consider to be the significance of your comparative analysis to you in your role as an L2 teacher.

Applying

A. Language Ideologies

Drawing on what you learned from your study of the linguistic landscape of your community, create an imagined linguistic landscape for your community or neighborhood. Once completed, construct a narrative (written or digital) that explains your choices of the types of representation and language(s) used in terms of their connections to your beliefs about language.

B. Language Policies

Create a set of explicit language policies for your classroom or the classroom in which you aspire to teach. Begin with a mission statement that clearly expresses your professional position toward language use in the classroom. In drafting your policies, consider the language(s) of instruction, including the language(s) that students are allowed to use during instruction, whether the policy will distinguish between the language(s) used between you and your students and those used among students and between official instructional times and non-instructional times. Once completed, share and compare with your classmates, and, together, consider the following questions:

- How similar/different are your policies?
- What accounts for the similarities/differences?
- How challenging was the process of constructing a set of policies?
- What implications can you derive from the process for your own teaching? For L2 teacher preparation?

References

Blommaert, J., & Backus, A. (2011). Repertoires revisited: "Knowing language" in superdiversity. *Working Papers in Urban Language & Literacies*, 67. Accessed 23 July 2012 at www.kcl.ac.uk/sspp/departments/education/research/ldc/publications/workingpapers/67.pdf.

Blommaert, J., & Rampton, B. (2011). Language and superdiversity, in *Diversities*, 13, Accessed 9 February 2014 at http://unesdoc.unesco.org/images/0021/002147/214772e.pdf#214780.

Cameron, D. (1995). *Verbal hygiene*. New York: Routledge.

Cooper, R. L. (1989). *Language planning and social change*. Cambridge: Cambridge University Press.

Cope, B., & Kalantzis, M. (2002). Introduction. In B. Cope & M. Kalantzis (Eds.), *Multiliteracies: Literacy learning and the design of social futures* (pp. 3–8). London: Routledge.

Cope, B., & Kalantzis, M. (2009). A grammar of multimodality. *International Journal of Learning*, 16(2), 361–425.

Council of Europe. (2001). Common European Framework of Reference for Languages. Retrieved from www.coe.int/en/web/common-european-framework-reference-languages.

Council of Europe Language Education Policy. (2006) *Council of Europe, Education and Languages, Language Policy*, Council of Europe, www.coe.int/t/dg4/linguistic/Division_EN.asp.

Creese, A., & Blackledge, A. (2010). Translanguaging in the bilingual classroom: A pedagogy for learning and teaching? *The Modern Language Journal*, 94(1), 103–115.

Creese, A., & Blackledge, A. (2014). Researching bilingual and multilingual education. In W. E. Wright, S. Boun, & O. García (Eds.), *The handbook of bilingual and multilingual education* (pp. 157–174). Malden, MA: John Wiley & Sons, Inc.

Creese, A., & Blackledge, A. (2015). Bilingual translanguaging: A pedagogy for learning classroom and teaching. *The Modern Language Journal*, 94(1), 103–115.

Creese, A., Blackledge, A., & Takhi, J. K. (2014). The ideal "Native Speaker" teacher: Negotiating authenticity and legitimacy in the language classroom. *The Modern Language Journal*, 98(4), 937–951.
Cummins, J., & Swain, M. (1986). *Bilingualism in education: Aspects of theory, research, and practice*. London; New York: Longman.
Douglas Fir Group (2016). A transdisciplinary framework for SLA in a multilingual world. *The Modern Language Journal*, 100, 19–47.
Farr, M., & Song, J. (2011). Language ideologies and policies: Multilingualism and education. *Language and Linguistics Compass*, 5, 650–665.
Flores, N. (2013). Silencing the subaltern: Nation-state/colonial governmentality and bilingual education in the United States. *Critical Inquiry in Language Studies*, 10(4), 263–287.
Flores, N., & García, O. (2017). A critical review of bilingual education in the United States: From basements and pride to boutiques and profit. *Annual Review of Applied Linguistics*, 37, 124–29.
García, O., & Kano, N. (2014). Translanguaging as process and pedagogy: Developing the English writing of Japanese students in the US. In J. Conteh & G. Meier (Eds.), *The multilingual turn in languages education: Opportunities and challenges* (pp. 258–277). Tonawanda, NY: Multilingual Matters.
García, O., & Leiva, C. (2014). Theorizing and enacting translanguaging for social justice. In A. Blackledge & A. Creese (Eds.), *Heteroglossia as practice and pedagogy* (pp. 199–216). London: Springer.
García, O., & Sylvan, C. E. (2011). Pedagogies and practices in multilingual classrooms: Singularities in pluralities. *The Modern Language Journal*, 95(3), 385–400.
García O., & Li, W. (2014). *Translanguaging: Language, bilingualism and education*. Basingstoke: Palgrave Macmillan.
Gorter, D., & Cenoz, J. (2017). Language education policy and multilingual assessment. *Language and Education*, 31(3), 231–248.
Haneda, M., & Sherman, B. (2016). A job-crafting perspective on teacher agentive action. *TESOL Quarterly*, 50(3), 745–754.
Irvine, J. T. & Gal, S. (2000). Language ideology and linguistics differentiation. In P. Kroskrity (Ed.), *Regimes of language: Ideologies, polities, and identities* (pp. 35–84). Santa Fe: School of American Research Press.
Kroskrity, P. (2004). Language ideology. In A. Duranti (Ed.), *Companion to linguistic anthropology* (pp. 496–517). Oxford: Blackwell.
Landry, R., & Bourhis, R. Y. (1997). Linguistic landscape and ethnolinguistic vitality: An empirical study. *Journal of Language and Social Psychology*, 16(1), 23–49.
Makoni, S., & Pennycook, A. (2007). *Disinventing and reinventing languages*. Multilingual Matters.
Makoni, S., & Pennycook, A. (2012). From monological multilingualism to multilingua francas. *The Routledge handbook of multilingualism*, 439.
McCarty, T. L. (2003). Revitalising indigenous languages in homogenising times. *Comparative Education*, 39(2), 147–163.
Miller, E.R. (2014). *The language of adult immigrants: Agency in the making*. Bristol: Multilingual Matters.
Milroy, J. (2001). Language ideologies and the consequences of standardization. *Journal of Sociolinguistics*, 5(4), 530–555.

Ortega, L. (2013). SLA for the 21st century: Disciplinary progress, transdisciplinary relevance, and the bi/multilingual turn. *Language Learning, 63* (Supplement 2013), 1–24.

Otheguy, R., García, O., & Reid, W. (2015). Clarifying translanguaging and deconstructing named languages: A perspective from linguistics. *Applied Linguistics Review, 6*(3), 281–307.

Phillipson, R. (1992). *Linguistic imperialism.* Oxford: Oxford University Press.

Piller, I. (2015). Language ideologies. In K. Tracy, C. Illie, & T. Sandel (Eds.), *The International encyclopedia of language and social interaction* (pp. 1–10). New York: John Wiley & Sons.

Rojo, L. M. (2015). The social construction of inequality in and through interaction in multilingual classrooms. In N. Markee (Ed.), *The handbook of classroom discourse and interaction* (pp. 490–505). Hoboken, NJ: John Wiley & Sons, Inc.

Shuck, G. (2006). Racializing the nonnative English speaker. *Journal of Language, Identity, and Education, 5*(4), 259–276.

Silverstein, M. (1979). Language structure and linguistic ideology. In P. R. Clyne, W. F. Hanks & C. L. Hofbauer (Eds.), *The elements: A parasession on linguistic units and levels* (pp. 193–247). Chicago: Chicago Linguistic Society.

Simpson, J., & Whiteside, A. (Eds.) (2015). *Adult language education and migration: Challenging agendas in policy and practice.* London: Routledge.

Tollefson, J. W. (2017). Language planning in education. In T. L. McCarty & S. May (Eds.), *Language policy and political issues in education* (pp. 17–29). London: Springer.

Tollefson, J. W., & Tsui, A. B. (2014). Language diversity and language policy in educational access and equity. *Review of Research in Education, 38*(1), 189–214.

Tsui, A. & Tollefson, J. (2003). The centrality of medium- of-instruction policy in sociopolitical processes. In J. Tollefson & A. Tsui (Eds.), *Medium of instruction policies: Which agenda? Whose agenda?* (pp. 1–18). Oxford: Taylor and Francis.

Wiley, T. G. (1996). Language planning and policy. In S. L. McKay & N. H. Hornberger (Eds.), *Sociolinguistics and language teaching* (pp. 103–147). New York: Cambridge University Press.

Wiley, T. G. (2014). Diversity, super-diversity, and monolingual language ideology in the United States: Tolerance or intolerance? *Review of Research in Education, 38*(1), 1–32.

Wiley, T. G., & Lukes, M. (1996). English-only and standard English ideologies in the US. *TESOL Quarterly, 30*(3), 511–535.

Woolard, K. A. (1990). Language ideology: Issues and approaches. *Pragmatics, 2*(3), 235–249.

Woolard, K. A., & Schieffelin, B. B. (1994). Language ideology. *Annual Review of Anthropology, 23,* 55–82.

Index

activity-based identity *see* social identity
affordance 49–50; modal affordance 50–52
agency 13, 115–116, 118
Atkinson, D. 3, 4

Bakhtin, M. 48–49
bilingual education programs 158; dual/two way 160; transitional 159
Byrnes, H. 4

Chomsky, N. 28
classroom interaction 131–134
cognitive abilities 7, 64, 66
Common European Framework of Reference for Languages 158
communicative repertoire *see* repertoire
competence 11, 31; communicative 28–29, 31; linguistic 28; multi-competence 29–30
complex adaptive system 25–28
constructions 24–25
Council of Europe 158–159

design 52, 55, 138
designing *see* design
digital literacies 128–129
digital story 121
directed motivational current 111
Doran, M. 4
Dörnyei, Z. 110–111, 117
Douglas Fir Group 4, 63
Duff, P. 4

Ellis, N. 4
embodied resources 85–86
emergent grammar 27–28

Five Graces Group 27
funds of knowledge 127

García, O. 39, 161
genre 82
gesture *see* embodied resources
Gumperz, J. 31

Hall, J.K. 4
Halliday, M. 82
Heath, S. B. 126
hegemony 157
Hymes, D. 28–29, 76–77

ideologies 9, 14
imagined communities 99–100, 113–114
imagined identities 12–13, 99, 102, 110
indexical potentials 80
indexicality 79; indexicals, indexes 80
interaction engine 63
interactional instinct 62–63
investment 112–114, 116, 118
IRF 131

Johnson, K. 4

knowledge processes 15–17, 37, 138

L2 motivational self system 110
L2 socialization *see* language socialization
language acquisition device 23, 28
language education policies 157
language ideologies 153; monolingualism 154–155; native speaker 155; standard language 153–154

172 Index

language policy and planning 156–158
language socialization 76–80, 86; L2 socialization 80–82, 86, 128; in schools 129–131
languaging 33
Lantolf, J. 4, 135
Larsen-Freeman, D. 4
Li, Wei 34–35, 161
linguistic competence *see* competence
literacy practices 13–14, 125–128

Matthiessen, C. 83
meaning potentials 48–52
mediation 78, 84, 86, 135–136
mediational means 78, 84–85
medium of instruction 157–158
mode 46, 50
Moll, L. 127
monolingualism ideology *see* language ideologies
motivation 109–110, 116
multi-competence *see* competence
multiliteracies pedagogy 15–16, 118, 138
multimodal ensemble 47–48, 55
multimodality 46–47

native speaker fallacy 155
native speaker ideology *see* language ideologies
Negueruela, E. 4
New London Group 15, 52, 138
Norton, B. 4, 97, 112

Ochs, E. 76–81
Ortega, L. 4

pedagogy of multiliteracies *see* multiliteracies pedagogy

register 52–53, 102
repertoire 11, 30–32, 36; communicative repertoire 52–54
role relational identity *see* social identity

salience 64, 66, 70, 136
scaffolding 134
schema of expectations 52
Schieffelin, B. 76–78
Schumann, J. 4
semiotic resources 5, 11, 24, 45–46, 82, 84, 96–97
social identity 8, 12, 95–101, 103; activity-based identity 95–96, 100–101, 102, 103; situated 95–96, 103; transportable 95–96, 103
social institutions 7–8
stance 79
standard language ideology *see* language ideologies
super-diversity 30, 53
Swain, M. 4
systemic functional linguistics 82

Tarone, E. 4
task-based language teaching 136
token frequency 65
transdisciplinary framework 3–5; macro level 8; meso level 7–8; micro level 5–7
translanguaging 33–36
translanguaging pedagogy 160–161
transnational literacies 129
transportable identity *see* social identity
type frequency 65

usage-based 23–24, 33, 160

Vygotsky, L. S. 83–85, 134

zone of proximal development 134–135